THE
GREEN WICCAN
MAGICAL
SPELL BOOK

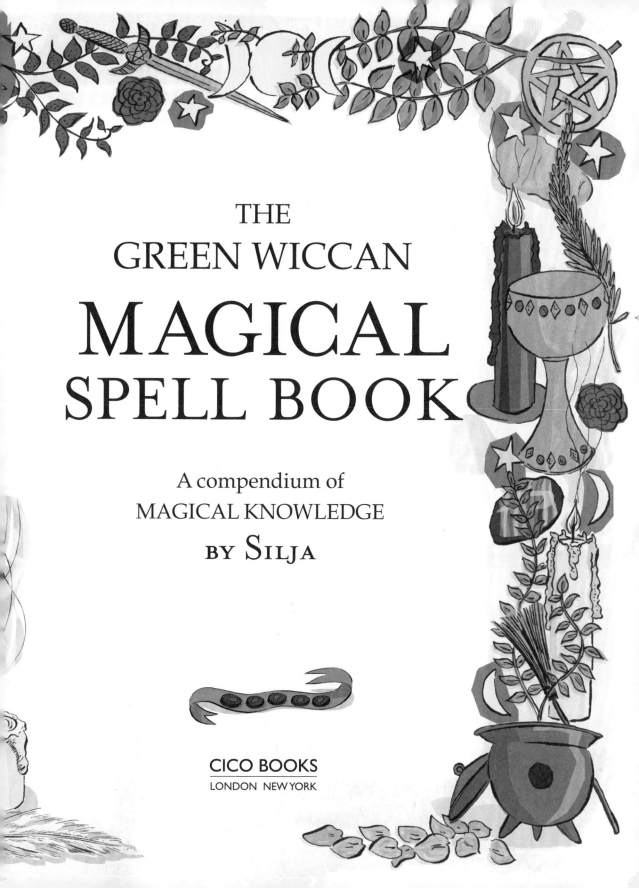

THE
GREEN WICCAN
MAGICAL
SPELL BOOK

A compendium of
MAGICAL KNOWLEDGE
BY SILJA

CICO BOOKS
LONDON NEW YORK

I WOULD LIKE TO THANK THE LORD ROBIN,
MY FIRST WICCAN mentor AND HIGH PRIEST, FOR HIS VALUABLE TEACHINGS;
THE COVEN OF THE SILVER WHEEL OF THE STARS AND ALL ITS MEMBERS PAST AND
PRESENT FOR THEIR FELLOWSHIP; AND MY WONDERFUL HUSBAND AND
THREE KIDS, JUST FOR BEING THEMSELVES.

This edition published in 2018 by CICO Books
An imprint of Ryland Peters & Small Ltd
20–21 Jockey's Fields, London WC1R 4BW
341 E 116th St, New York, NY 10029

www.rylandpeters.com

10 9 8 7 6 5 4 3 2 1

First published in 2011

A CIP catalog record for this book is available from the Library of Congress
and the British Library.

ISBN: 978 1 78249 659 5

Printed in China

Editor: Marion Paull
Designer: Roger Hammond
Illustrator: Michael A. Hill

SAFETY NOTE
Please note that the recommendations in this book are not intended to replace the
diagnosis of illness or ailments, or healing or medicine. Always consult your doctor or other
health professional in the case of illness.

Contents

Introduction

For years, loyal readers of my monthly spell advice and witchy teachings column in the magazine *Spirit & Destiny* have been asking for a book of spells. I try my best to answer everyone's emails, but do not always have time, so I realized that a book would allow everyone to look up magic whenever they like. But to be honest, I didn't want to compile a list of spells. Many such books already exist and I always feel they are lacking so much—spells do not work well if you don't know about their magical background and how to perform them. So this is the beginners' book I much preferred to write. It includes spells, but also has plenty of other information, to give a well-rounded introduction to Green Wicca, a modern tradition of Wicca, working in harmony with Mother Nature.

This was an interesting book to write, as I tried to pin down the most important teachings that I have focused on in my training coven's 15 years of existence, and then arrange them to fit into one book. It was hard to decide what to include and what to leave out, especially in Part One, Magical Theory and Practice. Part Two, Spells, was easier—thanks to my coven friends often asking for spells, and the feedback from readers of my *Spirit & Destiny* column, I knew which spells were the most successful for each topic, and selected those, together with a few brand new spells written especially for this book.

The little stars at the beginning of a spell ✪ signify its difficulty level. One star is for an easy spell that anyone can do; it doesn't require much concentration or experience, or any complicated ingredients. Two stars indicate a spell that may take some preparation; not an overly complicated spell, but it may not be suitable as a first spell, and could require some expensive or not-readily-available ingredients. Three stars mark a spell that is a bit more complicated and may suit a witch with some experience; it may use ingredients that are difficult to get. This doesn't mean you can't do a three-star spell if you are a beginner, but one- or two-star spells are more likely to work for you.

An interest in Tarot cards and doing guided meditations with friends started me on my occult journey, and I quickly became interested in Wicca as a religion and the practice of witchcraft.

Over the years, my practice has changed, going from eclectic Wicca through traditional Alexandrian Wicca and Celtic Wicca, back to a more "hedgewitchery" type of witchcraft. The great thing about this religion, and magic in general, is that it is so adaptable; it can change with your views, your experience, the time and money you have to devote to it, and anything else that influences your life. There are guidelines to morals and practice, of course, and some things work better for some people than others, but it is a wonderfully changeable religion, which I hope is reflected in this book.

ALL SORTS OF ALTARS

A great example of the adaptability of Wicca to different situations is the altar. Some of my friends are in the enviable position of having a ritual room with a permanent altar, completely dedicated to magic, but that is not necessary. I have a cabinet in the living room that I use as an altar and also to keep my witchy books, crystals, and other magical tools. Other coven members drape an embroidered altar cloth over the dining-room table, or use a windowsill, or improvize with a tree trunk in the woods at the back of the house. If you have it, use it; if you don't have it, don't worry about it.

I leave you with this blessing, and hope you enjoy the book:

May the sun high in the air
Give you the strength to dare
May the oceans of your soul
Be healed and make you whole.

This circle is open, and yet it is unbroken.
Merry meet, merry part, and merry meet again!

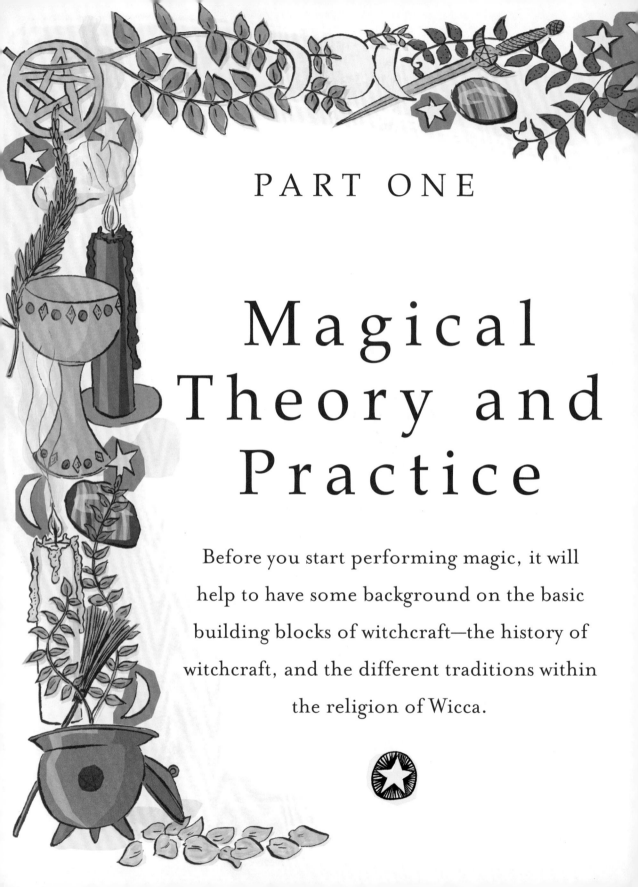

PART ONE

Magical Theory and Practice

Before you start performing magic, it will
help to have some background on the basic
building blocks of witchcraft—the history of
witchcraft, and the different traditions within
the religion of Wicca.

If what I have written about the history and current
state of witchcraft in Chapter 1 interests you,
I urge you to look at the resources page at the back
of the book for further reading.

Chapter 2, Magical Tips and Tricks, will get
you started on practicing magic and, I hope, help you
realize that you do not need to be a Grand Wizard
with tons of experience and expensive herbs and
crystals, or have extraordinary psychic powers, to
practice magic. All you need is an interest, an open
mind, and the willingness to learn.

CHAPTER 1

Background to Magic

To be able to perform magic successfully,
it is vital to understand how and why it works—and why it may
not work!—and when to tread carefully, so that you don't
endanger yourself or others. Staying within the moral
boundaries of spellcraft is essential.

This chapter will explain the theory and ethics of
magic, why and how magic works, and the different witchy
and Pagan traditions.

herbs

cauldron

broom

athame

witch's hat

rituals

Witch's pyramid

A four-sided pyramid symbolizes the Wiccan code and guides witches in their magical practice. The sides represent knowledge, willpower, daring, and silence.

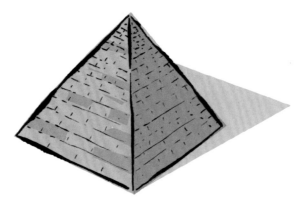

TO KNOW—intuition is important but so is research. Books and the internet are there for you to use, and talking to experienced witches is enormously helpful. At first, reading and hearing different opinions may be confusing, but from all that knowledge, you can crystallize your own beliefs and refine your practice.

TO WILL—you need strong will, both to gather the magical energy necessary to make spells successful, and sometimes to defend your beliefs. Positive thinking is a big part of magic. If you don't have the self-confidence to believe in it, your magic is unlikely to work. Witches have been known to be quite stubborn!

TO DARE—especially in the beginning, you will need to take risks and try spells without knowing how successful they are going to be. You will need to look inward to learn about yourself, and you may make some uncomfortable discoveries, but the process will help you to grow. You should always try to be as safe as possible, but without risk, there is no reward. Dare to question what you think you know, and dare to practice what you learn from this book!

TO BE SILENT—years ago, secrecy was more important than it is now for anyone practicing witchcraft, and Wicca still has some secret traditions, especially surrounding initiations. This side of the pyramid also reminds us not to be prideful or boast when our spells work. Sometimes, silent magic is most powerful, and can help us to focus our energy.

Magical ethics

Wiccans have often been accused of immorality because we don't believe that our bodies, or the Earth, are evil or sinful, as preached by most of the world's major religions. A line from the inspirational poem *Charge of the Goddess*—"All acts of love and pleasure are my rituals"—may seem to endorse that idea, but it doesn't actually mean that we have orgies. Wicca has values and ethics. Its two main guidelines for both performing magic and living spiritually are:

AND IT HARM NONE, DO WHAT THOU WILT

At first glance, this seems fairly easy, but it can be a little more complicated than making sure the herb you are going to use isn't poisonous. "And it harm none" refers not only to other people, but also to yourself, animals, plants, and the Earth. All are connected spiritually, ecologically, and physically, and we must carefully weigh our actions against their consequences, being guided by an awareness of the impact of our deeds.

The concept of black versus white magic comes from this principle. Basically, anything that goes against another person's free will, or is harmful, is considered black magic; beneficial spells are white magic. However, there is some controversy about this interpretation, since it isn't really the magic that is black or white, but the intent of the witch performing it.

LEST IN THY SELF-DEFENSE IT BE, EVER MIND THE RULE OF THREE

This one is a little easier. Think of karma, or reaping what you sow. Wiccans believe that what you do comes back to you threefold, so if you send out bad energy in the form of a spell or action, not only does it backfire on you, but you suffer three times the consequence! And if you have been deliberately harmed, the perpetrator will suffer the consequences sooner or later.

Why and how magic works

HIDDEN REASONS

Remember the line "Sometimes I thank the Lord
for unanswered prayers" (from a Garth Brooks' song). Maybe your
herbal spell or ritual isn't working, not because you did something
wrong, but because it is not right for you—for example, it may not
be the right time for you to move house or start a new relationship.

Magic has no certainties or guarantees; even an experienced witch won't be 100 percent successful. What it does do, though, is change probability. For example, if you do a spell to win the lottery, even if your chances double, they are still tiny (which is why you won't find any such spells in this book). But if you are one of three people up for promotion, doubling your chances with a spell will significantly increase your prospects of getting the job. Magic uses the energy of the universe. The herbs, colors, crystals, and other paraphernalia help because they have their own magical energies, but you are the main part.

So if a spell does not work, have a close look at all aspects of it: did you do it for the right reasons or were you selfish? Was the herb you used healthy and potent, or was it moldy, or weak in magical energy because it grew near a highway and was poisoned by fumes? Maybe you need to change the colors of the candles, or add to the spell by asking the blessing of a patron deity, such as Eros for love, Brigit for motherhood, or Ceres for wisdom. Did you try to do several spells at once, spreading your own energy too thinly? Also, think whether the spell may have worked without you realizing it, because you were closed to the possibility that the milkman could be your new lover, for instance; or perhaps it is taking some time to manifest itself; for example, it may be that your bosses are quietly earmarking you for promotion.

Sun and Moon

The sun and the moon have been worshipped since the
first members of the human race set foot on this Earth. They are equal
opposites, neither more important than the other, balancing each
other perfectly. The Moon Goddess and the Sun God are the
archetypal female and male energies. So, while some specific deities
represent them, the term "Moon Goddess" is often used to
mean all female deities, and "Sun God" all male deities.

The Moon Goddess is symbolized
by a triple moon (waxing for the
Maiden Goddess, full for the Mother
Goddess, and waning for the Crone), and
is seen as caring and cleansing; thus you
might ask the Moon Goddess for guidance
if you cannot see through a haze of
emotions or other obstacles in your path.
Think of the way the moon illuminates
even the darkest night.

The Sun God is usually symbolized by a
sun, or a simple yellow or orange circle.
He is seen as invigorating and energy
giving, so you might ask for his blessing
when your mood is downbeat, or you need
extra energy to carry you through a difficult
day, or to finish a
project at work.

FOLLOW THE SUN

To draw in the Sun God's energy, turn your
face to the sun, closing your eyes—never look directly at the sun—
and feel its warmth spread through you physically and spiritually.
Some famous Sun Gods to pray to while doing this are
Helios, Apollo, Ra, and Lugh.

The four elements

Earth, air, fire, and water are important in witchcraft. They constitute four of the five points on the pentagram (the fifth being spirit), and are called upon when casting a circle of energy before any ritual.

Earth

A feminine element, symbolized by a bowl of salt placed on the north corner of the altar, although on small altars space can be saved by adding salt to the water bowl in the west corner. This is usually done early in a ritual, to symbolize the balance and nourishing value of water and earth. Use a brown or green candle for earth. Its magical tool is the pentagram, which may be embroidered on the altar cloth or burned into a wooden disk, and its season is autumn, when Mother Earth yields most of her bounty. In rituals, earth is usually represented by wheat and oat sheaves, and potatoes, although any plant life could be used. The best time of day to work earth magic is in the freshness of morning; this is also the best time to see the animal representing earth, the stag, at the edge of your local woods.

Earth gods include Pan, Cernunnos, and Adonis, and goddesses are Demeter, Rhiannon, and Ceres.

Air

A masculine, easterly element that represents change. Air's season is spring, when warm winds bring hope for a new growing season, and its symbolic times are dawn and dusk. Its colors are white and yellow, and the wand is its magical tool. Air is associated with intuition—important in all aspects of witchcraft. This is helped by wafting clearing incense, such as sandalwood, around before you do a ritual or perform a spell. Travel magic, spells concerned with gaining knowledge, and magic or meditation aimed at contacting ancestors are linked with air. Birds are its key animals, and sand and diamonds its stones. Patron deities of this element include the goddesses Arianrhod, Lilith, and Aradia, and the gods Mercury and Thoth. No one food symbolizes air, but edible flowers may be used to decorate the altar, and eaten after a ritual.

Fire

The athame—a ritual knife, its blade forged in fire—represents this masculine element, and one is placed in the south corner of the altar. At bigger rituals, as well as having the flame of the altar candles, bonfires are often lit in the south. Fire is a symbol of balance and the circle of life, providing light and heat while at the same time being a force of death and destruction. It has a purifying, changing energy, making things better by warming, but destroying that which is old and no longer needed. Its season is summer and its time of day noon or early afternoon, when the sun is at its zenith—fire is closely associated with the Sun God—and the fire salamander basks on sun-warmed rocks. Its colors are red and orange, and it is represented by red bell peppers, and fiery foods such as chilies and mustard. More gods than goddesses are associated with fire—powerful deities such as Baal, Loki, and Agni. Brigit, Vesta, and Pele are fire goddesses.

Water

A feminine element, symbolized by a bowl of water placed on the west corner of the altar. The chalice is water's magical tool. This element is cleansing and purifying, seemingly a universally held belief since holy water and holy wells feature in ancient Celtic rituals and Roman Catholicism, besides other religions. Water's season is winter—snow is water after all—and its color blue or gray. A blue candle in the west of a room represents water. Rice, tuna, and seaweed are its symbolic foods, sapphire its stone. This element is often used in spells for emotional stability, to help with bereavement, and for cleansing and healing. Water deities are generally powerful, and some of them can be quite destructive. The more benevolent ones include Lir, Neptune, and Poseidon, and the goddesses Boann, Venelia, and Latis.

☗·TIP·☗

Pumpkin flowers floating in a bowl of water are a wonderful altar decoration. The water represents its own element, the flower stands for air, the orange color of the flower represents fire, and the pumpkin plant represents earth, so all four elements are portrayed together.

Mythology in magic

Wonderful mythological stories come from around the world, and I encourage all students of Wicca and witchcraft to read those from other cultures besides those of their ancestors. Wicca is a modern religion, less than a hundred years old, and these old stories can teach us about ethics, history, emotions, and how to cope with difficult situations, as well as about magical people and places. Plenty of them involve witches and magicians (just think of Merlin).

Mythology can also be used more directly in spells and rituals. Often mention is made of herbs, colors, and crystals. Dian Cécht, the old Irish healing god, used magical water from holy springs mixed with feverfew to heal the Tuatha De Danann after battles. Water from these springs is still regarded as curative, and feverfew is known as a healing herb to practitioners of alternative medicine and witches alike. For ancient Egyptians, color was important. Osiris was depicted with green skin to symbolize his fertility and prosperity, and Seth, the god of virility and guardian of fire, had red hair and eyes—the same reasons we use these colors in magic today.

Many Wiccan initiation ceremonies involve passage through the underworld— the world of death and ghosts—and being reborn, and so the story of the phoenix may be told around a bonfire, or the story of Persephone, or Orpheus, with the initiate as the main character. Mythology also plays a part in seasonal celebrations, known as Sabbats. For example, the May Queen—the symbol of spring, energy, and innocence—is crowned during the Beltaine Sabbat, on 1 May.

> ### LOCAL HELP
>
> It is always worth researching the history and mythology of the area where you practice magic; that way, it is easier to tap into the energy of Mother Nature, and contact local spirits for help.

Different Pagan paths

"Pagan", "Wiccan", and "witch" are often used interchangeably, but the terms have very different meanings. First of all, witchcraft is not a religion. As the name implies, it's a craft that involves magic, but that also works with the power of herbs and crystals, alternative medicine, astrology, mythology, and various methods of fortune telling. You do not have to be a Pagan to be a witch. I know Jewish, Christian, and even atheist witches!

FALSE NOTIONS

Wicca most closely resembles the Hollywood idea of Paganism, but the two are still miles apart. If you've picked up this book because you want to levitate and smite your enemies with lightning, you will be disappointed!

Paganism is an umbrella term for many different Earth-based spiritualities and religions, many, but not all, stemming from pre-Christian beliefs. The main ones are Wicca, Druidism, Asatru, Voodoo, Shamanism, and Hedgewitchery.

WICCA

By far the most well-known and popular of these Pagan paths is Wicca. Many traditions have evolved within Wicca (see page 21), based on varying practices and revering different cultural deities from Celtic to ancient Egyptian. However, these generally involve a coven led by a high priestess, and various stages of initiation. Spiritual gatherings (see pages 122–9) are called Esbats (for Full Moon rituals) and Sabbats (for larger festivals), and while they change with the seasons, they are usually quite similar each time.

DRUIDISM

A Celtic path, based on the pre-Christian practices and beliefs of the ancients living in the British Isles, Druidism tends to be more of an outdoor practice than Wicca, and puts greater emphasis on knowing Celtic mythology. Druidism is seen as male dominated, and while it does seem to attract more men than women, it is not a biased path.

ASATRU

This follows northern deities, such as Odin, Freya, and Thor. There are similarities to Druidism, but Asatruers tend to be more warrior like—although not violent—in their outlook, self-reliance, and the emphasis they place on honor and loyalty. Groups of Asatruers working together are called a hearth.

SHAMANISM

With fewer rules and traditions than the others, practitioners of Shamanism are often solitary, meeting occasionally to exchange experiences. Much of this spiritual practice is based on journeying to other planes of existence, such as the astral plane, through introspection, meditation, and working with totem animals. It is usually, though not always, associated with more exotic cultures, such as those from Siberia and various parts of Africa.

VOODOO

This tends to be darker than other Pagan paths, and sometimes involves animal sacrifice. It also calls for worship of Roman Catholic saints. The original practitioners of this path came as slaves from Africa to the Caribbean.

HEDGEWITCHERY

Sometimes called Kitchen Witchery, Hedgewitchery is probably the closest we come to the medieval "Wise Woman" type of witchcraft. It is not a well-defined path, but that is precisely what makes it popular!

People following this path concentrate on the *craft* aspect of witchcraft, seeking knowledge from different traditions, their ancestors, and people close to the local energy, such as farmers and the elderly. They often do not bother with the more ceremonial aspects, such as casting circles and wearing robes, and while some worship specific deities, many just believe in an undefined Higher Power and that "Everything is Magic and Magic is in everything!". It is a great path for beginners still trying out different ways of working, and suits the solitary witch perfectly.

Wiccan traditions

GARDNERIAN

Gerald Gardner, author of *Witchcraft Today*, is the founder of modern Wicca. The path named after him is extremely traditional, with a hierarchical grade structure (three degrees) and the requirement to be skyclad (or naked) for rituals.

Every member of a Gardnerian coven has to take an oath of secrecy, promising not to reveal personal details of other coven members, or some of what is happening at the rituals. Gardnerian Wiccans do not usually advertise their coven, and you may need to ask to join one several times, once you have discovered it, before they will invite you to do so.

ALEXANDRIAN

Alex Sanders was a famous Wiccan in the 1960s. He reformed Gardnerian Wicca to make it more suited to the hippy culture of the time, although it is by no means a soft option. Alexandrian Wicca tends to be more eclectic and liberal; for example, coven members may worship deities from different pantheons, and even new members may be encouraged to assist in rituals. Being naked is usually required for initiation rituals only. While confidentiality is expected, no oath of secrecy is taken.

DIANIC

This feminist version of Wicca can be traced back to the 1920s, and anthropologist Margaret Murray. It is a mixture of several traditions, but its focus is on female spirituality and the goddess, especially Diana. Most Dianic covens allow both men and women to join, but concentrate on goddess worship; some allow women only, though, as they feel men would oppress the women's spirituality.

CELTIC

The Celtic tradition, my chosen path, is based on the practices of the pre-Christian Celtic people of the British Isles and Europe, with the acknowledgment that there are many things from those days that we do not truly know about, or that are unsuitable for modern worship. These practices are mixed with some Alexandrian and Druidic elements, and while some rituals, or parts of rituals, are always the same, much of the Celtic tradition is adaptable to the season, and to the tastes and beliefs of coven members. This tradition is Earth- and nature-based, and strong in the religious aspects of Wicca.

CHAPTER 2

Magical Tips and Tricks

First of all, it is important to remember that tools, herbs, candles, gems, and so on are not actually necessary to work magic. Your own energy and the power of your mind, as well as the blessings of deities and spirits, are the important things. However, these extra ingredients do make it easier to work spells—and are undoubtedly nice to have—so this chapter is about spell and ritual equipment, and how to adapt ingredients if you cannot get rare and specialized items.

In the second half of the chapter, I show you how to adapt your magic. That is the wonderful thing about Wiccan magic—it is so flexible! Once you have adapted some spells, you are on your way to writing your own magic.

Candles

Natural tallow and beeswax candles are good, but all you really need are some plain white candles. You can change the color by using crayons; or you could tie a ribbon of the color called for in the spell around the base of the candle and from that it will take on the color's energy.

Essential oils

Essential oils are often used to anoint other items, such as candles or clothes. Often, the easiest thing to do if you cannot find the required essential oil is to go back to basics—instead of dabbing with clove oil, push a clove into your clothes; instead of rubbing basil oil on your candle, rub a basil leaf on it.

Sometimes, oil is necessary, though. Making your own essential oil is difficult, but you could make an infused oil. Use a simple, plain carrier, such as almond or olive oil. Put some in a small bottle, add your chosen herb, such as rosemary and leave this to infuse for one lunar month.

Magical tools

These are often given to coven members for initiations or Sabbats, and, of course, solitary witches miss out on this. You can often buy them inexpensively at witchy conventions or on the internet, but ordinary, nonwitchy shops can also be good places to look. For example, for pentagrams, check the clearance aisle of your local supermarket after Christmas for "Star of Bethlehem" items; cloth gift bags make great charm bags, or receptacles for your tarot cards; dried herbs are not ideal but may be easier to find and use than fresh, especially if you don't do a lot of herbal magic. Otherwise, it's easy to grow herbs in a small pot on your windowsill.

For cauldrons, look in garden centers for pots, or kitchenware stores for soup terrines. Besom brooms can be found in hardware stores. For robes, you can use old-fashioned nightgowns in plain white, purple (the color of occult knowledge), or your favorite color. Ideally, they should be made from natural fabrics, such as cotton or wool, and you could embroider them with sygils, your magical name or the names of deities, or other symbols.

Eye of newt and dragon's blood

No, you don't need to kill lots of reptiles or appeal to St George for some dragon's blood—many seemingly rare or impossible spell ingredients are much simpler to find than you may think! If you come across a spell that calls for something odd, do some internet research and you will often find that it's a plain ingredient. For example, dragon's blood is actually resin from a palm tree, used for magical writing, but since it can be found only in occult stores, use purple ink instead, or plain ink that you charge by leaving it out in the moonlight for a night and sunlight for a day. Eye of newt is actually mustard seeds, and bat wings are holy leaf, which you can probably find on a walk in the woods.

When all else fails

When you absolutely cannot find the right colored candle or make the right smelling oil, or are simply unclear about what is needed, use something plain, because that is pure energy and you can never go wrong with that. White as a color is always good, which is why new members in most covens wear white. Use white candles when in doubt. And a nonperfumed massage oil for anointing yourself, your wand, or other equipment will always work, although it may not be as potent as the specified one.

♦ TIP ♦

The reason traditions have become traditions, sometimes existing for centuries, is because they are known to work. But don't be afraid to go down another path if it works for you. For example, pink is the traditional color for romantic love, but if you have always associated pale green with love because your first love gave you a pale green scarf, then use that color in your love magic instead.

Making your own magical things

I am not very craft oriented, and don't have much time to spend on making my own tools and ingredients, but I still have quite a few homemade magical things. Some are easier to make than to buy, and others are significantly less expensive to make yourself. Here are some items you can easily make at home, even if you are not very talented with your hands.

PERSONAL MAGIC

Remember that what we are practicing here is witchcraft, i.e. a craft. By making your own ingredients, you infuse them with your own personality and energy, increasing their potency in any magic you use them for.

WANDS AND STAFFS

Go for a walk and find a branch from a tree you particularly like to make into a wand or staff. Hawthorn, hazel, oak, and ash are traditional, but you can use any wood that you feel drawn to. Faery branches—a branch with another wood growing around it in a spiral pattern—are especially potent and great for any kind of spirit and protection magic. There is no need to whittle and carve the branch unless you want to; just make sure it's completely dry. A wand's length is usually from your wrist to your elbow, and a staff should be more or less as tall as you are.

ROBES

For a simple robe, measure yourself from ankle to shoulder, and find or buy a piece of cloth (white is best, for pure energy) twice as long as this and as wide as your outstretched arms, wrist to wrist. Fold the cloth lengthwise, cut a hole in the middle for your head and use a cord of purple (for occult knowledge), or your favorite colour, to bind it at the waist. If you like, sew up the sides and take the robe in a bit at the waist, and use fabric paint to draw on magical sygils or a pentagram.

HOLY WATER

A simple way to make Wiccan holy water for cleansing and blessing items is to leave a bowl of spring water out under a full moon. Some famous Moon Goddesses are Artemis, Diana, Coyolxauhqui and, of course, Luna.

PENTAGRAMS

Draw a pentagram on a plain plate with a colored marker, or, for even more magical energy, use a suitable herb sprinkled in a pentagram pattern—cloves to fight negativity, peppermint to calm a situation, and cinnamon for love.

CANDLES

Candle-making kits are usually available from hobby and craft stores. They often suggest melting down the remnants of old candles, but do not melt down candles that you have already used for one spell to re-use in another spell—see "After Magic" below. The magical energies will clash! Making your own candles for magic is a great way to achieve the combination of colors you want—for example, for making good money and career decisions, make a candle with green for prosperity in the middle and blue for wisdom on the outside.

INCENSE AND CANDLE HOLDERS

You can make a stick incense holder from playdough, which has the added advantage of coming in lots of different colors! I also like using large beads or gemstones drilled for use in a necklace—my favorite is amber. For a votive holder, scoop out a fruit or a vegetable that's suitable for the magical work you are doing— for example, an orange for justice and to symbolize the Sun God, a red apple for love, a yellow apple for friendship.

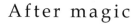

After magic

It is common to use up all the magical ingredients in a spell or a ritual—a candle burns down; a herbal tea is finished, But sometimes, you have ingredients left over, —for example, because you cannot let a candle burn unsupervised. What do you do with the magical ingredients then? Most importantly, do not re-use them! You can use the same candle or herb for the same spell over and over, but not for something else. The energies would clash, leading to strange, or no, results. The exceptions to this are the major ingredients, such as Tarot cards or gemstones used in a spell. You can cleanse these by burying them in coarse salt and passing them through or above the flame from a white candle, reblessing them with holy water, and leaving them for a while under a full moon and then in sunlight. However, try not to use such major ingredients again for at least one lunar month.

The best use for minor magical ingredients, such as herbs, candles, and pieces of cloth, is to give them to Mother Nature. Bury the candle stub or throw the herb into a river with thanks to a suitable deity—Venus for love, Cernunnos for inner strength, Diana for animal magic. Otherwise, you could use the item for nonmagical purposes, which will give whatever you do with it a hint of magic. For example, use the peppercorns from a bad-neighbor spell in cooking, which will infuse the food with magical energy; burn the red candle from a love spell as you invite your lover to visit.

TOO MUCH MAGIC?

Several spells and/or rituals and meditations are listed for most topics in this book; some of the more popular subjects, such as finding love or drawing money to you, may have ten or more aimed at achieving the same, or very similar, goal. That does not mean you should perform them all! It is generally best to concentrate on one spell at a time.

Unless mentioned otherwise, most spells should show signs of working within one lunar month (28 days), so if your first spell didn't work, I suggest waiting at least a month until trying a different one. Personally, unless it is an urgent issue, I like to wait three months. Similarly, don't perform too many spells on the same day, even if they are for different things, because this will sap your energy. Not only will you be worn out, but none of the magic will work well.

How many spells you should do depends on how difficult they are and how experienced and able to raise energy you are, but as a guideline, I would recommend one spell a day in your first year of working magic, two in your second year, and three from then on.

Magic and modern technology

Witches love using technology. For a while, when the World Wide Web was first developed, there were more Wiccan and Pagan sites out there than for any other religion! Now, members of some online magical groups organize themselves to perform the same magic at the same time— even mass rituals for Earth Day or to stop war—the idea being to pool all their magical energy. Many witches, including me, keep their *Book of Shadows* online for searchability and ease of sharing with friends and coven members.

☗·TIP·☗

A magical computer deserves magical protection. Before adding files of spells, smudge your computer with dried sage, and keep an amethyst near it to absorb negativity and to prevent the computer from crashing. When the stone goes dark or pale, bury it in coarse salt for a lunar month, then leave it basking in moonlight for a night and sunlight for a day before using it again. I always have one amethyst in use, and one charging like this.

Mobile phones can be used for magic, too. You can set reminders for the full moon, and send yourself texts to help with positive thinking or cosmic ordering. For example, if insecure in a new job, program your phone to send you a text just before work starts every morning, saying, "I am a knowledgeable, successful person. I deserve this job and I will impress people!"

Use a magical chant or song by a Wiccan group as your ring tone to remind you of your spirituality, and protect your phone with a colored cover— a blue one to boost your health and prevent the phone from breaking, or a green one to increase prosperity.

Magical names

You don't need to have a magical name to be a witch, but it
helps you to distinguish between your mundane self going about your
daily activities, and your magical self, who meditates and
performs rituals.

There are many ways to choose your
magical name. Some people just know what
is right for them, maybe after coming
across the name in a book on Wicca
or mythology, or when talking to
other Wiccans. Others meditate
at length (see pages 109–10),
asking for guidance from deities,
spirits, or ancestors, and feel they
are "given" a name. Alternatively, you
could use the numerology of your birth
date or mundane name to find your
magical name; or if you have a shortlist of
a few names you like, ask the Tarot cards, or
pendulum, for guidance.

WHAT NAME CAN BE USED?

Whatever you feel like! Some witches like to
choose the name of a favorite deity, but, to
me, that feels disrespectful. You can never
live up to the name (would a Christian call
themselves "God"?) Many witches choose a
hero from mythology, or a first name that
means something special, such as
Ursula, meaning strong female bear.
Others look to their heritage and
choose a name in the native language
of their ancestors, or they might
combine two or three favorite things,
such as a color and a herb, or a season, a
tree, and a crystal. Yet others take the name
of their totem animal, or recently deceased
familiar, as their magical name. There's no
reason why you can't just make something
up—a collection of letters that forms a
pleasant sound—or change it later after
a major life event or initiation alters your
spiritual path, or simply as you get older
and your first chosen name no longer
seems appropriate.

WHAT'S IN A NAME?

In the old days, when witches were persecuted, a magical name not
only helped you to connect with the deities and in your magical work,
but also protected you against being hunted and possibly killed, since
no one, not even fellow coven members, knew your real name.
Thus no one could betray you, not even under torture.

Adapting spells

Everyone has an individual magical energy or "footprint," and the great thing about magic—and Wicca as a religion—is that it is adaptable! You should consider adapting the spell you want to perform to your own needs and abilities. Once you have some experience, it is a good idea to adapt some spells as a stepping stone to writing your own magic.

How to adapt magic is totally up to you. If a spell calls for casting a magical circle with a wand, you could cast a simple circle with your hands instead; or find a nice branch from an oak tree to serve as an instant wand; or make your own by tying together some twigs of herbs with a suitably colored thread.

If you feel a color correspondence is wrong, visualize the color in a simple meditation. For instance, if green, which traditionally stands for prosperity, doesn't feel right for you, see a bubble of green energy dancing in front of you. How does it make you feel? Look closer at the energy ball. What do you see in it? Maybe you can see objects or events from your past that explain why you think green doesn't stand for prosperity, but for love, or something else.

If a herb ingredient in a spell feels wrong, look back to see if you associate it with an event in your life. You could also research its mythology in various cultures, especially if you feel drawn to a specific pantheon of deities, as herbs and colors are often interpreted in different ways.

·TIP·

To learn about magic and figure out your own preferences, find some spells from the internet and adapt them so they work for you; or so you think they would work—no need to perform them all! You can use silly, over-the-top spells for this; it's purely an exercise to help you find your own path.

MAGICAL TALISMAN

Instead of doing a spell, you can incorporate the ingredients into a talisman.
By carrying it with you or wearing it, the magical energy should stay stronger
for longer. If you already have, say, a four-leaf clover or a special coin you could
add some extra magic by keeping it in a colored pouch; for instance, keep your
lucky coin in a green pouch for prosperity.

If you don't already have a talisman, it's easy enough to make one from scratch.
Here are a couple of options:

Take a small pouch of a suitable color, or stay with white, which is good
for energy; add some gems and/or herbs to suit the purpose, and a symbol
of what you are trying to achieve. Leave it out in the sun for a day and in
moonlight for a night; then keep it where it is needed—under the sofa for
a talisman to guard against family fights, for example.

Find a wooden disk with a hole in it, or a locket, which you fill
with a thin layer of suitably colored wax. Inscribe the disk/wax with a symbol
representing your magical intent; for example, a house if you are trying to find
a new home, or a rune or a Sanskrit letter. You can even make your own sigils by
creating an abstract symbol with all the vowels taken from the word that
describes what you are trying to achieve—the O and E from love,
for example. Once a day, make a knot in a cord or ribbon of a suitable color,
while visualizing the spell's goal. At the end of the week, thread the
amulet on the cord or ribbon and wear it against your skin.

Writing your own magic

Getting started

First of all, think about whether you really need a spell. Sometimes, performing magic seems to be an easy option when the alternative is working hard to achieve the result you want. But while it may be tempting to consider using a spell that takes ten minutes rather than studying for hours, remember that magic actually takes a lot of time to prepare properly, and it also takes spiritual and mental energy (see "When not to use magic", page 135.) Since this is the case, be choosy and don't just use magic for any small problem you face.

Once you have decided that magic is your best option, and you know what kind of spell you want to perform—do you need healing, are you drowning in debt, does your relationship need strengthening?—think carefully about your precise intent. Say you decide that your debt problem is the one you will work on magically. Do you want to perform magic to lessen the debt, which is a very specific spell, or to gain a raise at work, which is a little less specific? Is a general spell to draw money to you what you have in mind?

When to cast a spell

Magic is powerful, and a spell will always have some energy, no matter when it is performed, but it will work better if you choose an auspicious time. There is no

hard and fast rule about this. For example, you might decide that Friday is the best day to perform your new love spell because it is dedicated to Venus and so is the traditional

☊·TIP·☊

If you have limited access to spell ingredients, and to witchy shops or online supply stores, base your spell on what you can find. This is good practice for writing spells, because it forces you to think about what you can do with what is available to you, and hones your creativity and resourcefulness.

time to work love magic. But if you are trying to attract a man, you might choose Sunday instead, since the day of the Sun God is great for dealing with male energies. The tables of magical associations at the end of this book (see pages 136–7) are an easy guide to help you decide on when your spell will work best.

Phases of the moon

Taking note of the phases of the moon is probably the most important factor in magical timing, whether for spells or rituals, and even for some meditations. The moon symbolizes the Mother Goddess, and together with the sun, balances the sky. We all know that the moon has a gravitational pull on the Earth, causing the ocean's tides, as well as people to behave differently. Apparently, more customer service complaints are received around a Full Moon, and more babies are born.

Wiccan covens usually meet monthly at or around the Full Moon, and schedule ceremonies, such as initiations or handfastings, for a blue moon, which is when two Full Moons occur in a calendar month.

The moon has four primary phases—new, waxing, full, and waning—and several secondary phases, such as the quarter moons and the Dark Moon. For magic, usually only the four primary phases are important. That being said, if

🕯·TIP·🕯

An easy way to figure out if the moon is waxing or waning is to remember the triple moon symbol—the waxing moon on the left represents the young maiden, growing toward the full moon in the middle, which symbolizes the Mother, and she in turn will become the waning moon on the right, representing the Crone.

you have written a spell and feel it is perfect, but it just doesn't work quite as well as you intended, maybe perform it toward the end of the waxing moon rather than at the beginning, or make other slight time adjustments, such as performing the spell at dawn rather than later in the morning. Also note that witches consider the New and Full Moon to extend over the two or three nights and days during which the phase seems to last, not just for the single night when they are signified astronomically.

NEW MOON

For two or three nights in each cycle, the moon isn't visible in the sky at all. This is the New Moon, and it is governed by the Maiden Goddess. The appearance of the new crescent moon is celebrated as a return of the moon from the dead. Hence, this is the ideal time for new beginnings and to start long-term projects. Good spells to do now include those to help you tread a new spiritual path, to encourage a relationship, and to make new friends. Fertility magic is also indicated.

WAXING MOON

The phase between a New and Full Moon is referred to as the waxing moon or, sometimes, the right-handed moon. This is firstly because the crescent looks like the shape made by your right thumb and forefinger, and secondly because this is the time for growing and positive magic. Good spells to do now include those to help you gain money or find love, and to improve your health. It is also an auspicious time for magic aimed at a job promotion.

FULL MOON

The moon is round in the sky for two or three nights in each cycle—the Full Moon, governed by the Mother Goddess. This is when the moon's power is at its strongest, and it is a time of abundance and completion. So, it is the best time to put the finishing touches to a project, or to schedule a long-term spell to end. Good spells to do now include blessings for a house, a new magical tool, or a relationship. This is also the time to give thanks for those spells that worked.

WANING MOON

This phase, between the Full Moon and the New Moon, is associated with the Crone. It is sometimes called the left-handed moon, because the crescent looks like the shape made by your left thumb and forefinger, and also because diminishing or lessening magic is done now. Good spells to do at this time include those to lose weight or reduce debt, to get rid of negative emotions or bad luck, and to heal the body from an illness.

Composing a spell

I find the easiest way to write a spell is to create it as you would a food recipe. First, make a list of ingredients, and write down any pre-conditions—is the spell to be performed on a specific day of the week, for example, or during a certain moon phase? Then explain what to do, step by step, not forgetting even the smallest steps, such as lighting a candle. (It makes quite a difference to a spell whether a candle is lit throughout, or only at the end in order to burn something in the flame.) Explain what to do with each of the ingredients listed. Should a herb remain on the altar, or be burned? If salt or sugar is to be sprinkled around another object, such as a photo or a candle, should this be done clockwise (to increase energy) or anticlockwise (to diminish energy)?

If there is a vocal component to the spell, write this down, too. Most spells with a vocal component rhyme. This is partly because it is traditional, but also because rhymes are pleasing to the ear, easier to memorize, and can help with the energy of the spell. But the words don't need to rhyme if you prefer them not to.

RHYMING SPELLS

Spoken spells always used to rhyme because when witchcraft was illegal, it was dangerous to leave evidence around in the form of a Book of Shadows. All spells were handed down orally from High Priest or Priestess to coven members, and rhymes are easier to remember than long sentences.

CHOOSING THE RIGHT WORDS

Think carefully about the wording of your spell. Even if you are angry about a bully, don't use swear words, because this will only reflect badly on you. Also consider including a caveat to protect yourself and the target of your spell from any unintentional egotistical feelings and wrong intentions. A caveat may be something like the traditional

"As above, so below,"

which is basically asking for the universe to provide balance with the spell; or

"If it not be for the good of all, I wish this spell to fail."

At the end of your chant, or at the end of the spell, you may want to include a power word or sentence, to seal your spell and send it out into the universe to work its magic.

The traditional wording for that is:
"As I will it, so mote it be!"; or *"By the power of the moon/this magic will work soon/by the power of the sun/this spell's begun!"*; but you could say something as simple as *"Now!"*

An easy way to combine your caveat and the power sentence is to say:
"For the good of all, and the harm of none, this spell be done!"

Keeping your own Book of Shadows

In the old days, each witch had a personal "grimoire," or Book of Shadows. Often, after a new member had been initiated into a coven, he or she would be given access to the High Priestess's Book of Shadows, and expected to copy selected parts, or maybe all of it, by hand. It was considered a great honor to be given access to all those spells and to so much handed-down knowledge, and ensured the new coven member had a good basis on which to build his or her own grimoire.

Many witches still keep their own journal, because there is something special, and very spiritual, in writing down your own spells in your own hand in a book.

You can choose an ink color suitable for each spell—write your health spells with a blue pen, your love spells in a red crayon (or dragon's blood ink), and so on. If you choose to have a paper Book of Shadows, I would strongly recommend that you compose your new spells on loose pieces of paper or in a spiral notebook first. That way you can make changes if necessary. After the first time you perform the spell, for instance, you may feel it should be done on a different day, or perhaps using a different herb.

Of course, we live in the modern world and one of the great things about witchcraft is that it seamlessly integrates tradition and ancient wisdom with modern knowledge and abilities. So, many witches keep their Book of Shadows on a computer, which makes it easier to amend spells if you find you have made a mistake, and to share your magic with coven members

☗ · TIP · ☗

Although there's no longer any need to fear persecution for performing spells, you may have some personal spells that you'd like to keep secret. If so, you could write them in lemon juice, or in a different language.

and online friends. It also makes searching for that particular banishing spell or ancestor ritual easier.

If you choose to have an electronic Book of Shadows, you should protect it from prying eyes by using a password, even if you are the only one using that computer. This not only protects your privacy and the spells you have worked so hard to create, but it also prevents misunderstandings that might occur when people read something that has been taken out of context.

Having your Book of Shadows on the computer also means you can add information as you go along. Every time you perform a spell, note the details of when you performed it, the moon phase, where you got the herb from, and any special circumstances.

Even seemingly minor things can be important. The telephone ringing could have been distracting, even though you didn't answer it; or a pigeon landing on your windowsill just as you blew out the candle could affect the outcome.

One lunar cycle after you performed the spell, check for results. Of course, you can do this earlier or later, but most spells take less than a month to work if they are going to, so checking after a lunar cycle is a good guide.

PART TWO

Spells

Many of these spells are from my
personal Book of Shadows. I wrote them
for myself, for coven members, or for
others to perform, and they have proven
to be successful.

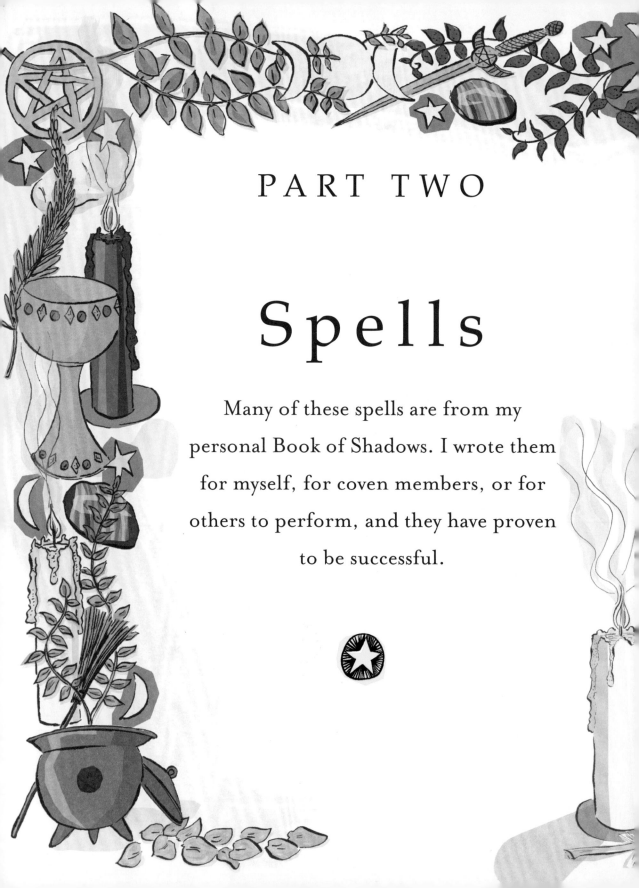

If you are new to witchcraft, or unsure about
working magic and performing spells, it would be a
good idea to read Part One of this book first, which
explains the theory of how magic works, the ethics
to keep in mind when working it, and also what some
of the more esoteric ingredients are and how to get
hold of them, or substitutes for them.

I do, however, try to keep my spells simple
and not use complicated or expensive ingredients.
For a note about the "star" rating system, see page 6.

Magic is always most powerful when you
put lots of your own energy into it, so if you plan
on performing spells regularly, it is worth having
some basic ingredients to hand, so they can soak up
your personal energy in your home.

CHAPTER 3

Love Spells

You can use a love spell to encourage love, or to
strengthen existing love in someone, and it is okay
to do a general "find love" spell when you have someone
specific in mind. But a spell should never go against
a person's free will in an attempt to make them love you;
that would not be true love anyway, and could end
in tears for everyone.

In this chapter you will find

spells to help you:

⬦ fall in love and settle down

⬦ make relationship decisions

⬦ spice up your sex life

⬦ enjoy a calm and loving relationship

⬦ let go of love

vanilla

cinnamon

candles

rose quartz

red and pink

rose petals

Useful ingredients

Some basic love-spell ingredients come up time and again,
and so are always good to have in the house if you need to write or perform
some love magic. I would recommend:

ROSE QUARTZ—in raw form or on jewelry, but preferably as small pebbles because they are versatile and can be given away.

CINNAMON—most people have this in the house, and it can be used for love, lust, and virility spells.

VANILLA—fresh vanilla pods can be expensive and difficult to find. Vanilla essence and vanilla essential oil work almost as well, and are easily obtained.

RED AND PINK ITEMS—have some red items on hand for vigorous, lustful,

passionate love, and pink for more romantic, settled love. Paper and scraps of cloth are great; clothes and underwear if you mostly do spells for yourself.

ROSE PETALS—roses are a symbol of love, red for passion and pink for romance; a white rose with a pink blush or pink tips to the petals is good for spells. If you grow roses in your garden, you can harvest the petals and dry them yourself.

CANDLES—red and pink are what you need, but, failing that, white candles can be given pink energy with a pink crayon or ribbon.

To find love

✪ To attract love in a general sense, I recommend wearing a round rose quartz—maybe carry a pebble in your pocket or wear a ring with an oval or heart-shaped rose quartz. To strengthen this basic spell, wear the rose quartz next to your skin.

☆ ☆ ☆

✪ Before you go out, put on some vanilla or cinnamon-based scent, but rather than

applying it directly to your skin, spray a cloud in front of you and step into it while saying:

"Love comes to me, I am stepping into my loving future."

☆ ☆ ☆

✪ Bake shortbread cookies in the shape of hearts, adding some vanilla essence for romantic love. Just before they are ready, sprinkle them with cinnamon, for closeness and strengthening love, and brown sugar for the sweetness of the relationship. Brown sugar is also balancing and down to earth. Give the cookies to the subject of your affections on a Friday, which is Venus, the love goddess's day, or Sunday, which is sacred to the Sun, for male energy.

☆ ☆ ☆

♥♥ At night during a waxing moon, light a pink candle. Gaze into the flame and think about what you are looking for in a man, and where you might find it—by joining a sports club, or becoming more involved in your religious community, or just getting the word out to female friends that you are looking. Then say:

"Fire with you I sow
True love that I not yet know.
Soon will come the day
When true love comes to stay.
Make my and his heart blaze and shine
To bring a relationship so fine
And bless with true love this heart of mine."

Blow out the candle, kiss it three times, and then put it away. Do this spell once a week until you have established a promising relationship.

☆ ☆ ☆

♥♥ Shortly after a new moon, take a red ribbon to a willow tree (NOT a weeping willow!). Select a young, supple branch and twist it into a knot, visualizing yourself with the person in question. Then tie the red ribbon to the branch, once above and once below the knot. Next time you go for a walk together, make sure you walk past the willow tree. If the branch is still securely knotted with the ribbon around it by the next full moon, you will be a couple within a month.

☆ ☆ ☆

♥♥ Rub a rose quartz stone with cinnamon oil and wear it on a gold chain next to your skin, ideally at the level of your heart. The gold represents the sun and is to attract male energy.

☆ ☆ ☆

♥♥ Hold a rose quartz pebble in your left palm (the left guides intuition) and with your right thumb (for making sensible decisions), rub a drop of cinnamon essential oil (cinnamon is a potent love herb) into the pebble while chanting:

"Where love may be found, no one can tell
But I hope to find it with this magic spell!"

Carry the rose quartz with you always, as you never know where love may be found!

☆ ☆ ☆

♥♥ Take a pink candle, for romantic love, and rub into it some cinnamon essential oil or cinnamon powder. Light the candle every Friday, Venus's day, and say the following five times:

*"Fire of this candle, hereby I sow
the best love I shall ever know.
Make my heart be filled with love
and affection.
From betrayal and false love, let there
be protection.
As the flame of this candle does shine
let true love be mine!
Soon I trust will come the day
when real love comes to stay."*

Then, blow out the candle, and put it away
until the next Friday.

☆ ☆ ☆

✪✪ Buy some cinnamon mints. Wait for a
clear night on a waxing moon. Make a small
box from pink cardboard, or line the box of
mints you purchased with pink paper. Say:
*"Silver moon, shining bright
Send to me my Mr Right.
I'm looking for that loving link
To make my life and heart go pink.
I have these cinnamon mints
So banish the toads and summon my prince!"*

Carry the mints with you wherever you go,
and offer one to any prospective partner.

To find settled love

✪ Cut out a heart shape from red
paper—or pink paper if you'd rather
have romantic, old-fashioned
love—and write in it all that you want
from a new man in your life (be
realistic!) Keep the heart somewhere safe
and quiet until you are in a relationship,
when you can burn it, and give thanks to
the deities for their help in finding love.

☆ ☆ ☆

✪✪ On a small piece of paper, and using a
black pen, write down the five worst
qualities of men you have known. Really
think about this. Then flush the paper
down the toilet, and as it disappears,
visualize men who are bad for you staying
away from you. Next, get another piece of
paper, and with a pink or red pen, write
down the five qualities you really look for
in a good man. Sprinkle some cinnamon

on the paper, then fold it three times
to contain the cinnamon, and with each
fold say:
*"Love and happiness come to me,
as I will it, so shall it be!"*

Keep this paper in your bedroom until you
have found someone to love.

☆ ☆ ☆

✪✪ Pair a rose quartz with an
amethyst, which provides
stability and also promotes
your psychic senses, helping
you to figure out intuitively if someone is
right for you. Ideally, find a piece of
jewelry featuring both stones, or carry one
of each in the same pocket, so they touch.

☆ ☆ ☆

✪✪ Rub a piece of rose quartz, deosil (clockwise), with vanilla oil every morning at dawn, while looking at the sunrise.

☆ ☆ ☆

✪✪ Buy a pink bra, or add a pink ribbon to a white bra. Vanilla is a love spice, which will attract eligible men, but its pod is black, which absorbs bad energy from past relationships. So rub a vanilla pod over the bra before you wear it, chanting:

"Bad men I want none,
heartache be gone!
I seek partnership and love ,
I ask for blessings from below and above!"

Wear this bra whenever you might meet suitable men.

☆ ☆ ☆

✪✪ Each Friday, Venus's day, and Sunday, day of the Sun god, mix a teaspoon of cinnamon with a pinch of ground red pepper. Dip your finger in the mixture and draw a heart on your forehead while saying:

"Like a beacon will shine
this heart of mine,
Love I will find
this spell I hereby bind!"

Repeat every Friday and Sunday until you are in a steady relationship.

☆ ☆ ☆

✪✪✪ Rub a piece of rose quartz deosil (clockwise) with vanilla oil once a week. While you rub the stone, visualize yourself happy with a husband by your side and children running around. Say the following chant three times:

"Love and happiness I seek
So that my future is no longer bleak.
A man and children in my future I see
Please guide me to them, Powers that be!"

The timing isn't crucial for this one, but it's best to do it at dawn, while looking at the sunrise.

To make a decision

✪ To figure out if someone you like is right for you, get a deck of cards and take out the Queen of Hearts. This card represents you. Place this card in front of you, then shuffle the rest of the deck while thinking about the person. When you feel ready, slowly turn over the cards. If he/she is right for you as a long-term, partner, the King of Hearts will be within the first 25 cards. If the relationship is going to be exciting and fun, the Jack of Hearts will be within the first 25 cards. If the Jack turns up without the King, it looks like a short-term affair.

If the King of Clubs shows up before either of the other two cards, then even if there is to be relationship, it will be a troubled one; it's up to you to decide if it's worth it.

☆☆☆

♡♡ This spell will hone your intuition and help you make the right decision about who to date if you are in the enviable position of having two suitors.

Take four equally sized pieces of white paper—white for neutrality—and one red and one pink pen. Write each man's name on two of the pieces of paper, once in red, for passionate love, and once in pink, for romantic love.

Turn the papers so you cannot see the names and mix them up with your left hand, because your left hand guides your intuition.

Think of various scenarios in your future, such as a summer holiday, going to see your parents, being upset about work, your next birthday. After imagining each scenario, let your left hand pick one of the four pieces of paper. See who you picked, and how you feel about being with that person in that situation.

☆☆☆

♡♡ Again, to decide between two suitors, on a new moon, take three pieces of white paper and on two of them, with a blue pen—blue for wisdom—write one of the names, and list that person's good qualities in one row and bad qualities in another row. Leave the third paper blank. Fold each of the papers four times while saying:
"Lord and Lady help me see,
with whom I am meant to be.
Guide my hand and guide my heart
So my love may have a good start!"

Leave the folded papers somewhere safe until the full moon; then shuffle them while repeating the chant four times. Open the top paper. This is who you are meant to be with. If it's the blank one, you are meant to stay single for a while.

To spice up sex

♡ One simple way is to put a lighted red candle on your bedside table and try for some "alone time" with your partner around noon!

☆☆☆

♡♡ If you want your partner to be more exciting sexually, start with food. Make a risotto, or a pasta bake, with red bell peppers for virility and butternut squash for energy from the Sun God. As you stir in these vegetables, chant the following:
"Excitement we've had none
But now, boringness be gone!
Excitement and energy I seek
Fun we'll be, no longer meek!"

☆☆☆

❂❂ Rub some cinnamon essential oil into a red candle while thinking about ways to spice up your love life. It is great if your partner agrees to do the same, but not necessary. Then light the candle on the nightstand before you go to bed.

☆☆☆

❂❂❂ Make two dollies with fresh, green corn husks and red string, and write your name on one and your partner's name on the other. Place the dollies together somewhere safe; by the time they have dried out, your relationship will have grown more passionate.

To promote calm love

❂ Create harmony by adding some honey to hot milk and stirring deosil (clockwise) before serving it to your partner.

☆☆☆

❂ To increase love between you and your partner, display photos of the two of you together around your home.

☆☆☆

❂❂ To help with communication and to reduce arguments, wear a piece of amber into which you have rubbed a drop of geranium oil, or a piece of lemongrass, deosil (clockwise) while saying:

"We will talk friendly and with love.
Gods and Goddesses, bless us from
above.
Keep us together, keep us safe.
Help us remember the love you gave!"

☆☆☆

❂❂ Tie a blue ribbon—blue for wisdom—to the base of a yellow candle—yellow for friendship

and communication. Light the candle and chant the following nine times:

"I ask the blessings of Those Above for this talk
between me and [name], whom I love.
We will both speak and be heard
Respect each other and be truthful in deed
and word.
Bring us closer together
loved ones forever!"

☆☆☆

❂❂ Find a photo of the two of you happy together. Just after a full moon, place a black candle—to burn away negativity—in front of the picture, and light it for a few minutes every day, while remembering your happy times together. Once the new moon comes around, replace the black candle with a white one, to increase your joint energies and happiness. Visualize the two of you together in the future, maybe sitting in your favorite coffee shop while you recount what's happened in your life since you quarreled.

To strengthen relationships

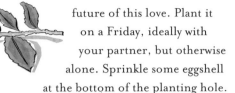

✪ Burn a vanilla-scented candle in the bedroom, or bake some cookies flavored with vanilla pods.

✪ Find two similarly shaped rose quartz pebbles, and sleep with them under your pillow for at least a week. Give one to your love and ask him to put it under his pillow wherever his travels take him, so you can be together in your dreams.

☆☆☆

✪✪ If you'd like the relationship to be more settled, put a photo of yourself and a separate photo of your partner in an empty crab claw, wrap the claw in pink cloth—for romantic love—and leave it under your bed.

☆☆☆

✪✪ To remove worries about a relationship, find a photo of yourself at a wedding and rub the back of it lightly with clove oil, to dispel curses and negativity. Let it dry. Then, with a pink pen for romantic love, write:

"[Your name] and [partner's name], very much in love and getting married soon."

Place the photo in an album or frame, and keep it somewhere safe.

☆☆☆

✪✪ Buy a red-flowering perennial plant with strong green foliage, such as a peony or a hollyhock. Green represents the fertile future of this love. Plant it on a Friday, ideally with your partner, but otherwise alone. Sprinkle some eggshell at the bottom of the planting hole. The egg is a symbol of fertility and of coming full circle, which you are doing by reconnecting with the happiness you used to have with your partner.

Water the plant regularly, while thinking about your relationship. When you have a drink of water, leave some water in your glass and use that, because it has your energies in it; use your partner's unfinished water, too. As the plant grows, so will your love for each other.

☆☆☆

✪✪ Just after a full moon, place a photo of the two of you happy together behind a blue candle—blue for healing and wisdom. Light the candle for a few minutes three times a day, while you imagine the bad feelings and communication difficulties between the two of you floating away.

At the new moon, replace the blue candle with a pink one—pink for romantic love—and light it three times daily while you think about your love growing stronger, and the two of you being happy again like you once were. After a month, your relationship should be much improved.

☆☆☆

✪✪ At the next full moon, intertwine a few of your hairs with a few of his—braid them if long enough. Wrap a white cord around the hairs. White is neutral, so it will not make someone love you, but it strengthens existing energies.

Look at the full moon and think about all the happy times you have had in the past, and the happy times you will have in the future.

Keep the hair somewhere safe, such as in a photo album with pictures of the two of you, or with a love letter he sent you.

Whenever you feel lonely, or have a normal tiff, look at the moon and think of him. You could ask him to do the same.

☆ ☆ ☆

✪✪✪ Place your favorite angel card, or a picture or drawing of an angel, in front of you, and put a photo of you and your partner happy together in front of it.

Crush some dried pink roses, red carnations, and peppermint, and sprinkle that mixture in a deosil circle around the two cards.

Take some time to think of all the happy times you have had together, and ask the angel to guide your feelings and protect your love.

Then, take a pinch of the flower mixture and place it under the bed you share or under the table or sofa where you sit together.

To let go of love

✪ Write down all you want to say about the relationship, using a black pen on cleansing white paper. Take it to a fast-moving stream, say this:

"Goodbye I say,
never again, I pray,
Sadness now I am letting go,
Cast it away, let it flow!"

Then, put the paper in the water and watch it float away.

☆ ☆ ☆

✪✪ To help you say goodbye, sit in the middle of a room quietly. Imagine the person you are splitting up with sitting opposite you, and envisage that you are linked by a silver cord. Think about all the experiences you have had together, good and bad. Cry and laugh if you want to, and take as long as you need.

When you feel ready, take a pair of scissors and move as if to cut the cord between you while saying three times:

"In love and light, I let you go."

Repeat this once a week until you feel better and that your bond has been diminished.

CHAPTER 4

Money and Work Spells

The key to success with money and work spells is to be realistic. Remember that magic changes probability; it doesn't make anything certain. Spells aimed at winning a fortune in a national lottery are unlikely to work since even if your chances are increased, they remain minute. It's a good idea to add the waiver *"And it harm none, this spell be done"* at the end of your chant—you don't want a money spell to work by your grandmother dying and you being in her will!

In this chapter you will find

spells to help you:

⋄ face your financial worries

⋄ draw money to you

⋄ bring money into your home

⋄ get a job

⋄ run your own business

⋄ deal with problems at work

Useful ingredients

Some basic money and work spell ingredients come up time and again, and are always good to have in the house in case you may need to perform some financial magic. I would recommend:

MONEY—like attracts like, and many money spells involve a few coins. Copper tends to work best, in my experience. Many witches suggest that money which has been used for magic should not be spent, but given to a charity after the spell has been successful.

GREEN ITEMS—green is the color of prosperity, so all kinds of green things are useful for financial magic, from candles and ribbon to folders to keep your documents in.

HEALTHY PLANTS—green leaves, especially round ones, shaped like coins, are symbolically powerful, and soil stands for Mother Earth's bounty.

GOLD—wearing gold jewelry while performing money magic is good, but the gold doesn't have to be real. Consider using gold foil chocolate wrapping, or gold candles, or other such things.

TIGER'S EYE—this golden brown stone is ideal for money and business magic since it consists of two money colors—gold for finances and brown for prosperity.

PEPPERMINT—great for dispelling negativity and stress in a work environment, because it is green and smells nice, peppermint also has a calming effect.

MOON WATCH

Pay attention to the moon's phases. Whenever possible, deal with reducing debt on a waning moon, so that as the moon gets smaller, your debt gets smaller. Tackle boosting the amount of money coming in—asking for a raise, selling items online—on a waxing moon, so that as the moon gets bigger in the sky, your money increases, too.

To face financial worries

✿ To lessen the stress of debt, and the problems financial worries can cause in a relationship, as you are writing checks and putting them in envelopes, say:

"Spirits, I ask our finances to bless, money shall grow, debt become less."

☆ ☆ ☆

✿✿ To help you and your partner understand where your money goes, and each other's financial priorities, use this spell.

Take a three-foot long green ribbon or piece of cloth and lay it out somewhere where it can remain undisturbed.

Starting on the day after the next full moon, each evening exchange a coin of the same value with your partner. You should smile at each other, then lay the coins on the green ribbon. Do this for a full lunar cycle.

During the waning moon, your missunderstandings and disagreements about money will decrease; during the waxing moon, your communication about money issues and agreement about how to manage finances will increase.

When there is a full moon, take all the coins you have collected during the month and do something as a couple, such as going to the theatre or having a picnic with a good bottle of wine.

You can repeat this spell as often as you like, when you feel you still have issues to work through, or simply if you enjoy the ritual of saving money and then spending it together.

To draw money to you

✪ This is a great spell to do at Samhain (October 31, the witchy New Year), on New Year's Eve, or at any Wiccan Sabbat.

Place a coin on your forehead and say the following nine times. If you can finish before the coin falls off, you won't have any financial worries for the next year:

"Lord and Lady come to me,
This year I seek prosperity.
I will work hard and clever
in debt I shall be never."

WEARING AN EMERALD

✪ To draw money to you, wear an emerald ring on your right hand, or a piece of emerald in a golden pouch over your sternum, starting on the day after a new moon, and wear it for at least one lunar month.

✪✪ For this spell, first clean three coins with mineral water. While you are doing this, imagine removing any emotional, physical, and mental negativity that may stop you from gaining more money. Imagine all your financial problems being washed away as the mineral water cleanses the coins. Then, arrange three basil leaves beside each other, and place a coin on each one. As you put each coin on the leaf, say:

"Gold and green,
little money I have seen.
I draw money to me,
for the best this may be!"

Then, eat the three leaves, and put the coins in your pocket. Make sure that at least one of the coins always stays with you, and it will draw more money toward it.

✪✪✪ Rub basil oil into a green candle on a Thursday—use a basil leaf if you have no oil, and you can always color a white candle green with a marker pen. Light the candle, breathe slowly, and visualize paying all your bills easily, and having enough money to live comfortably. Don't imagine having millions; this spell won't work if you are greedy! Say the following:

"By the powers of air, fire, water, and earth,
I release this spell. God and Goddess,
don't let me hear the debtor's bell!
For enough money to live I ask,
I'll take on any job, any task.
With harm to none, this spell be done."

Then blow out the candle and put it away. Do this every Thursday until you have the amount of money you need.

To bring money into your home

THURSDAYS ARE IMPORTANT

To attract money to your home, eat something containing basil
on Thursdays—add some to a salad, curry, or risotto, or drink herbal tea.
Also, pay bills and settle debts on a Thursday. This is the day of
Mars and the best time to deal with money worries.

✿ Plant some basil near your front door or keep a basil plant in a pot near your front door. Make sure the plant is healthy and does not have any dried or rotten leaves.

☆☆☆

✿ Place three copper coins under your front doormat to invite money into the house; do not disturb the mat until the needed money has been received.

☆☆☆

✿ Hang a perfect golden corn on the cob near your front door. Ensure there are no missing or discolored kernels.

☆☆☆

✿✿ On nine consecutive days, light a green candle, and chant the following spell nine times:

*"Money I don't need much
just enough for bills, food, and such.
For the good of all, and with harm to none
Lord and Lady, let this be done!"*

☆☆☆

✿✿ Place a few coins in a half crab shell and leave it where the sun can shine on it. Do not disturb the crab shell until the next Wiccan fire festival—Beltaine (May 1), Lughnasa (Aug 1), Samhain (Oct 31), or Imbolc (Feb 2)—when you should throw the shell into the fire with thanks to your patron deities for their financial blessings.

☆☆☆

✿✿ On a tiny piece of paper, write the amount you need, then roll it up tightly. Make a small hole in the top of a white egg—white stands for energy and purity of purpose, and the egg for prosperity—and push the piece of paper in. Bury the egg under a healthy green plant, preferably basil, but any healthy green plant will do.

As the egg's contents gently seep out and nourish the plant, helping it to grow, your financial situation will improve.

☆☆☆

✿✿ Surround a green candle with a tiger's eye bracelet or several small tiger's eye stones. Light the candle daily and visualize money coming to you. When you blow out the candle, say:

"And it harm none, so mote it be!"

✪✪ Light a green candle. Take a walnut and open it gently, so the two halves, and the nut inside, remain intact. Drip some green wax into each half. Place a small coin on top of one half, and quickly push the halves together. Hold the walnut between your hands as it cools, while thinking about how you will increase prosperity in your home. For example, think about asking for extra training at work to get a promotion, doing an evening course, or studying harder at college. Leave the nut somewhere safe, such as on your altar or on a windowsill in a quiet room.

To get a job

✪ Before bed, burn a green candle and say out loud your wishes for your next job. Then, blow out the candle and watch the smoke disappear, carrying your wishes with it. You may dream about ways to find your new ideal job.

☆ ☆ ☆

✪ On a green candle, scratch a list of the work you would like and are qualified for. Light this candle when you are looking through job ads on the internet or in newspapers or journals, when you are writing your resumé, and when you are getting ready to go for interviews. If it's possible for someone to light the candle while the interview is going on, so much the better, but do not leave a burning candle unattended.

☆ ☆ ☆

✪ While waiting for a job interview, or to see your boss about a promotion or raise, say this little chant under your breath:

"I am good in this job, you will see,
for opportunities and rewards, pick me!
Success I will find,
this spell together I bind."

☆ ☆ ☆

✪✪ Light a green candle at dusk, cross your hands behind the candle flame, palm on palm, and chant the following three times:

"I seek a job which fulfills
I seek a job which pays the bills
Help me find what I need
for happiness and not for greed!"

Look at your palms through the flame, in the same nonfocused way you'd look at a Magic Eye picture; relax your breathing. Inspiration on where to find the ideal job will come to you.

☆ ☆ ☆

✪✪ Place a large paperclip next to a green candle. Light the candle daily from the new to the full moon (as the size of the moon increases, so will your money and job

55

COLORS MATTER

For interviews, wear dark blue, because this color is calming and portrays confidence. Accessorize with understated gold jewelry, which attracts money and prosperity, or with something red, such as a scarf or pendant, which shows you are energetic and positive.

---

opportunities). Then say:

*"Financial troubles brought me low,
but a good job awaits me, I know.
In the past, times have been lean,
in the future, money will bring this
candle green!"*

Let a drop of the wax fall onto the bottom of the clip. By the end of two weeks, there will be a blob of wax on the clip. Put a brand-new note into the clip and carry this with you to interviews and the job center.

✫ ✫ ✫

✪✪ To figure out what to do jobwise, put a lighted green candle on your bedside table. Look into the flame and ask your favored deities to guide you in your career search. I recommend Vulcan, Roman god of work, or Epona or Lakshmi, goddesses of prosperity and happiness. Blow out the candle and keep a pen and paper by the bed, so that you can write down any dreams.

✫ ✫ ✫

✪✪ Take a green candle and scratch three words on it that for you symbolize a great job. It could be anything from "money" or "outdoors" through "creative" and "close by". Light the candle and spend a few minutes praying to your favorite deity for guidance. Then, spread out the job section of the newspaper; tilt the candle and let a few drops of wax drip onto the page. Apply for jobs that have the green wax on them, even if they seem out of your league.

✫ ✫ ✫

✪✪ With a green pen, make a list of all the jobs you can do, and a realistic goal salary. Fold the paper three times, saying each time:

*"As above, so below, for the good
of all and the harm of none, so mote
it be!"*

Put the paper at the bottom of a pot, cover with soil, and plant sunflower seeds. As the flowers grow, so will your job prospects. You should have a well-earning job by the time the first sunflowers bloom.

To run your own business

✪ Very few people become overnight successes. If you are branching out into the arts, take a copy of your best work (not the original!) and burn it. Mix the ashes with powdered cloves (to remove negativity) and grated nutmeg (to attract success). Then add a tiny pinch of this mixture whenever you send out a copy of your work. Rub some on your computer screen before sending electronic copies.

☆ ☆ ☆

✪ To help with selling a business, paint the front door green to draw solid buyers, and have some green, round-leafed plants near the front door. Wrap a piece of clear quartz (to increase energy and draw attention) in gold paper or gold cloth (to get the best financial return you can), and place this under the "For Sale" sign while you say the following five times:

"Money we need, business we lose.
Buyers, don't be obtuse!
We'll make it easy for you,
come and buy this place, do!"

☆ ☆ ☆

✪✪ Wear a tiger's eye stone near your throat. To give it extra power, say the following chant each morning while looking at it in the mirror:

"I am strong and wise,
my business will grow in size.
Independent and happy I'll be,
financial happiness come to me!"

PLANTS FOR AN OFFICE

Dark green, round or oval-leafed plants are ideal for an office. The roundness promotes harmony, the green symbolizes prosperity, and they give out lots ofoxygen. Make sure to clip dead leaves regularly to avoid them attracting bad luck.

To deal with problems at work

✪ Wear amber to absorb negativity and promote a positive work environment.

☆ ☆ ☆

✪ To ease tension in the office, make a cup of peppermint tea and make sure the smell and steam waft around the room. This will help dispel strife and negativity.

☆ ☆ ☆

✪ Keep cacti on your desk. Their phallic shape and prickly nature give vigour and make you stronger and more self-assured —useful in a role such as sales.

CHAPTER 5

Luck and Justice Spells

Balance is very important in Wicca, and the spells
in this chapter all address an imbalance in life. They are aimed
at promoting justice, for yourself or those who cannot help
themselves, achieving success with good luck, and removing
negativity, but they will not make you a winner unjustly. A success
spell alone will not guarantee that you pass a test if you do not study;
a justice spell will not give you sole custody, if this is
not right for the child.

In this chapter you will find
spells to help you:
✧ be more successful in tests
✧ attract good luck
✧ remove negativity
✧ discourage bad people
✧ encourage truth telling
✧ seek justice

orange

cloves

black

nutmeg

amethyst

coral

Useful ingredients

Some basic luck, justice, and antinegativity spell ingredients
come up time and again. Keep some at hand in case you need to perform
some magic to regain balance. I would recommend:

ORANGE ITEMS—orange is the color of justice. Have some orange candles, or crayons to transform white candles, and to write with.

CLOVES—these are an inexpensive and easy way to keep bad energy, and people, at bay. Buy whole cloves from the supermarket. Clove oil is also useful for the same purpose.

BLACK ITEMS—black absorbs negative energy the way it absorbs light. While black candles are not normally seen on a Wiccan altar, they are very useful for spells, as are black ribbon and cloth. Many Wiccans keep their magical things, especially Tarot cards, in black cloth to prevent them from absorbing negative energy while not in use.

NUTMEG—this is a great attracter of good luck. Keep a whole nutmeg and grate it as needed; that way it is fresh and more powerful than powdered nutmeg.

🕯 ·TIPS· 🕯

✪ To banish negativity and attract luck, keep a small goddess statue made from coral in your home.

✪ When reading a book about magic or attending a witchcraft class, wear a piece of amethyst to aid your study.

✪ Place some red clover flowers in individual ice-cube trays, add water, and freeze for magical ice cubes that you can add to any drink to attract luck and prosperity.

To encourage success in tests

A GOOD LUNCH

An egg and sweetcorn sandwich, or soup, will keep your energy levels up while you are studying. The sweetcorn helps you to retain information while the egg symbolizes success.

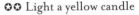

✪ To help you with a driving test, or any practical examination, dab a few drops of a favorite scent on a white handkerchief— white stands for pure, positive energy. When your practice goes well, and also when you feel generally relaxed and happy, close your eyes, sniff the handkerchief, and say to yourself:

"I can do this, I will do this, driving is fun.
I can do this, I will do this."

Do the same thing just before your test.

☆ ☆ ☆

✪✪ On the night of a full moon, light a white candle, and hold a gold coin between your flat palms. It doesn't need to be real gold; it can be wrapped in gold foil. Touch your forehead with your palms and say:

"On this right and ready hour I call upon the Moon Goddess's power.
By this sacred fire, bring to me my heart's desire.
By this coin of gold, all I seek will now unfold."

Then touch your mouth, throat, and heart, saying the same thing.

☆ ☆ ☆

✪✪ Light a yellow candle bedside your study desk, and when you feel yourself starting to panic, spend a few moments looking into the flame. Also, look into the candle flame when revising and memorizing information. Write this chant at the beginning of your study notes for each subject, and repeat it before each test:

"Lord and Lady, make me clear of sight,
Come forth to fill my mind with wisdom bright,
To keep my mind alert and clear,
I know I have nothing to fear
With this learning I ask, may my senses be keen.
I write these words to come into being."

☆ ☆ ☆

✪✪✪ To aid your studies, keep a sliver of emerald in your text book or with your lecture notes, and put it in a bottle to take with you to the test. This will help you to remember what you've learned, and to write it down eloquently.

To attract good luck

✿✿ Any small item can become a good-luck charm—a coin, a stone, a spoon or even a scarf or a handkerchief. If you don't already have such an item, you could buy a lucky gem, such as an adventurine or a black onyx. Each morning gently rub your left thumb over it while chanting the following three times:

"Bad energy go away,
I will not despair,
I will force negativity to tear.
Thoughts of happiness, thoughts of love.
Make me lucky, I ask the deities above."

Carry your lucky charm with you wherever you go.

☆ ☆ ☆

✿✿ Run a warm bath and add three teaspoons of grated nutmeg and a little almond oil. Say the following three times, submerging yourself fully after each chant:

"I have had much bad luck
my life is a suck.
But goodness and positivity
happiness, too, will come to me!"

While still in the bathtub, pull out the plug, and watch the water drain away, imagining your worries and bad luck disappearing with it.

GOOD LUCK GIFT

One easy way to transmit extra luck when sending a gift is to rub the cut edge of a whole nutmeg over the parcel. Another way is to make sure some blue is involved, either wrapping the gift in paper with a blue background, or tying it with blue ribbon, or maybe adding a small blue bauble for decoration. Blue stands for wisdom and healing, both physically and emotionally.

To remove negativity

TURQUOISE INDICATOR

If you are unsure of another person's intentions, wear a piece of turquoise jewelry next time the two of you meet, and ensure it is clearly visible. If the stones grow warm, that person wishes you well; if they go cold, the opposite is true.

✪ Write all your bad luck and problems on a piece of paper. Put on an old shoe and stomp on the paper three times. Then, burn the shoe in a fire, and bury the paper, wrapping three whole nutmegs in it. By the time the paper has dissolved into the earth, your problems will have gone away.

✪ Put a lemon quarter in the four corners of each major room in your house, while saying:

"The bitterness of lemon, like negativity's venom, fly away, be now gone; lemon's yellow shine, like the sun."

Leave the lemon slices where they are until they start turning black; then bury them away from your home.

☿ · TIPS · ☿

✪ Carry five whole cloves in a right-hand pocket to help ward off curses and to remove general negativity.

✪ During busy and worrying times, carry a large, rounded hematite pebble onto which you have placed three drops of lavender essential oil. Whenever you feel under pressure, slowly rub it deosil (clockwise) with your left thumb.

✪ If you can't stop thinking about a former partner, have a long, warm shower and wash your hair with a geranium or sandalwood-based shampoo—literally "wash that man out of your hair!"

✪✪ Cut an apple in half and hollow out most of the flesh. Write down all the bad things that have happened, using a blue pen on white paper—blue for healing, white for peace—and ask the Lord and Lady to rectify the situation to everyone's satisfaction.

Fold up the paper, put it into the hollow apple and tie the fruit back together with a black ribbon—black to absorb negativity. Eat the flesh that you scooped from the apple, thinking about how your life will change for the better and only good things will happen.

Then, bury the apple in the earth, preferably somewhere you pass by everyday, such as in your front yard. As the apple and paper disintegrate, Mother Earth will take the negative energy and curses and recycle them into good energy.

☆ ☆ ☆

✪✪ Collect as many red leaves as you have bedrooms in your house. Lay them in a circle, and place a blue candle in the middle. Light the candle and visualize yourself and your family happily reading, working, and restfully sleeping in your home. Say the following five times, and then blow out the candle, and place one of the leaves in each room:

"Red leaves, gift from earth,
Birth to death and death to birth,
Keep all evil far away,
Day to night and night to day."

☆ ☆ ☆

✪✪ Fill your cauldron with water. Place a black candle in it so that about an inch of the candle remains above the water. Light the candle and chant the following nine times:

"Curses, negativity
Leave me now, let me be!
You can no longer do me harm
You will no longer cause alarm."

When the candle flame touches the water, it will be extinguished and with it, any curse that has a hold on you.

PROTECTION FROM NEGATIVITY

On a gold chain, wear a clear quartz crystal so that it touches your skin at the level of your heart. From the crystal you get power and energy; the gold also gives you energy, and the protection of the Sun God.

To discourage bad people

✪ On the night of a waning moon, write the annoying or energy-draining person's name in orange crayon on white paper—orange for justice, white for peace.

Roll the paper up and submerge it in a small container of water, which you should then place in the back of your freezer where you don't need to disturb it. This will freeze that person out of your life symbolically and actually.

This is not an instant spell and could take several months to work completely, although you should see some results within a month. When the problem is solved, flush the frozen paper down the toilet.

☆ ☆ ☆

✪✪ Find a pendant in the shape of a strong animal, such as a bear, an eagle, or a panther. Choose an animal you like or, if you're doing the spell on behalf of someone else, a bullied teenager for example, let that person choose. Rub a drop of clove oil into the pendant widdershins (anticlockwise) while saying:

"Bad people, negativity stay away!
I will be safe and happy, I say!"

Then take a drop of your, or the subject's, favorite perfume—otherwise use sandalwood, which is a strong, protective scent—and rub that into the pendant deosil (clockwise) while imagining yourself or the subject safe and happy in a bubble of white, positive light. Give the pendant to the person for whom you are doing the spell if you think he or she will wear it. Otherwise, hang it over a photo of them.

☆ ☆ ☆

✪✪ Take some gray paper and, with a black pen, write down all the bad things that have happened in past relationships. Take some time—days or weeks if you like—to think about these things and how they have sapped your energy and confidence, and how you deserve better.

When you are ready, burn the paper, gather the ashes, put them at the bottom of a flowerpot and plant flowers in it. You could decorate the pot with hearts, or paint it red, if you are dealing with love relationships; embellish it with houses and stick figures for familial relationships.

I recommend sunflowers because they are easy to grow and they represent the Sun God—a strong, caring male deity.

As your flowers grow, you will find strength to move on and find the love you deserve.

To encourage truth telling

✿ A magical way to encourage someone to tell the truth is to put something given to you by that person, such as a CD, a letter, or a photo, in a pot and plant parsley on top of it. Parsley is a truth herb and it will encourage the person to speak the truth, and foster truth in your relationship.

☆ ☆ ☆

✿ At dusk, light a fire. List your problems, including any gossip or rumors that concern you, using a black pen—black for negativity.

Fold the paper three times, reciting the following each time you fold it. Then, toss the paper into the fire.

"Gossip, slander, nasty people tout,
with this spell, I cast you out!
I toss their words into the fires,
They will clearly be seen as liars.
All the evil that they say,
Make it all go away!"

☆ ☆ ☆

✿ If you find that someone is lying to you, lean a photo of that person against a blue candle—blue for wisdom and truth—light the candle and say the following spell three times:

"Earth of the North, nourish the truth,
Three times three, set them free, set them free.
Wind in the East, clear the air,
Three times three, let them see, let them see.
Fires in the South, burn the lies,
Three times three, set them free, set them free.
Water of the West, cleanse, let lies rest,
Three times three, let them see, let them see."

Repeat this spell every three days until you feel the person has stopped lying.

☆ ☆ ☆

✿ To come to a just compromise, carry five grains of barley and five grains of wheat when going to meet the person with whom you are negotiating.

(I have heard of a modern version of this using breakfast cereal!)

To seek justice

> ### COURTING JUSTICE
>
> If you have to go to court, place a piece of hematite over your heart and visualize the outcome that is right and just.

✪ Wear something orange when seeing your lawyer or going to court. Orange stands for justice. As you are getting ready, say:

"I am meek, but today justice I seek.
For the good of all, injustice will fall!"

☆ ☆ ☆

✪ Use an orange marker pen to draw an arrow pointing upward on a white candle. The arrow is the rune for justice. Burn this every time you talk with your legal representative and before you go to court.

☆ ☆ ☆

✪✪ To help you make the right decisions and to foster civility and cooperation in those around you, rub some amber with two drops of geranium or peppermint oil while saying:

"The right decisions we will seek.
We will be strong for children and
the meek!"

Do this every Monday morning, and carry the amber with you, preferably where it can be seen.

☆ ☆ ☆

✪✪ If a friend owes you money, draw an upward-pointing arrow on a white candle with an orange crayon. Stand the candle on top of a coin—you may want to secure it with a little wax so it doesn't fall off. Place a photo of your friend behind the candle—better still, a happy picture of the two of you together—and once a week, ideally on a Thursday or Saturday, light the candle for a few minutes while you visualize your friend giving you back the money. You should also light the candle whenever your friend is at your home.

☆ ☆ ☆

✪✪ To encourage a positive outcome of a court case, place a copy of the court papers on the table. Draw an upward-pointing arrow on a white candle with an orange crayon, and add the case number, or the name of the judge dealing with it, if you know that. Light the candle, place it on a saucer or plate, and then carefully put it on top of the papers. Look into the flame and visualize a positive outcome. Do this for five minutes every day until you get the result. Prepare a new candle if the first burns down completely. If you have part of a candle left, bury it in the ground.

CHAPTER 6

Home and Relationship Spells

The home spells will help you transform your living quarters to suit your personality and energy, which is important if you plan on doing spells there. Protecting your space, and those within it, is paramount, but it is equally important to move on without leaving emotional energy behind. The friends and relatives spells will help you to ease uncomfortable relationships. They will not force someone to be friends with you, because friendship by force amounts to magical or emotional blackmail, and is no friendship at all.

In this chapter you will find

spells to help you:

✧ cope with problem neighbors

✧ cleanse and bless your home

✧ sell your home and find a new one

✧ nurture and repair friendships

✧ take care of your family

✧ look after your pet

sage

white feathers

black peppercorns

black candle

turquoise stone

bell

Useful ingredients

Some basic ingredients are always good to have on hand in case you may need
to perform some homey magic. I would recommend:

**DRIED SAGE/SMUDGE
STICKS**—a quick and easy way to dispel
negative energy and cleanse a room is to
scatter dried sage or use smudge sticks.
This practice comes originally from
Native American beliefs but has
been carried over to Wicca.

WHITE FEATHERS—
a symbol of air and inspiration,
feathers are used a lot in magic.
White feathers symbolize peace and
waving away negativity.

BLACK PEPPERCORNS—these
can be used in magical potpourri, witch
bottles, or as part of a cleaning mixture
to protect your home.

BLACK CANDLE—light one of these
to burn away resentment from
neighbors, signal to ghosts they should
move out, or just burn away
negativity and stress after a fight in
the home.

BELL—a small hand bell with
a clear sound forms part of an advanced
altar set-up, but may also be
used in home magic, mostly
symbolically to cleanse the
house of bad vibrations
and energy, and to call
upon ghosts to leave.

EVIL-EYE CHARM

Is your child afraid of monsters in the wardrobe
or under the bed? If so, have your child draw an eye
on a smooth turquoise pebble, and put the
stone where the monsters are lurking. Explain
that it's a magical charm against the evil eye
and will protect them from monsters
and all negativity.

To cope with problem neighbors

✿ Make a mixture of four tablespoons of coarse salt, one tablespoon of ground black pepper, and 11 cloves, then add vinegar to make a thick paste.

Put some of this along the boundary line between your property and that of your troublesome neighbor— you can always say it is to discourage slugs if you are asked.

☆☆☆

✿ Gather some white feathers and tie them to fenceposts to promote peace with the neighbors.

☆☆☆

✿✿ When a neighbor is coming to visit, place three black peppercorns in a small box, such as a matchbox, and fill in equal parts with coarse salt and sugar.

The peppercorns represent negativity, coarse salt represents the sea washing away trouble, its whiteness neutrality, and sugar is for the sweetness of life.

Close the box, and visualize closing the lid on the troubles in your home. Put it in a safe place and do not disturb it until the visit is over, when you can throw it away. Make a new one for the next visit.

☆☆☆

✿✿ On the Full Moon, carve your neighbor's name into a black candle, and encircle it with some cloves.

This must not be disturbed for a while, so do it on a windowsill in a quiet room, or, if necessary, on a plate that can be moved into a cupboard during the day.

Light the candle for a few minutes every day, thinking about the bad behavior of the neighbor lessening.

On the New Moon, replace the black with a white candle, again with the neighbor's name scratched on it. Light it every day until the Full Moon, thinking about relations between the two of you becoming civil and nice.

If necessary, you can repeat this spell for several months, although you should see signs of things getting better after one or, at a maximum, two months.

☆☆☆

✿✿ Mix up mineral water, lemon juice, geranium oil, and vinegar, and use this to wash your house's floors and windows and polish door frames. You can even spray it on outside walls.

This will banish any bad feelings and negative energy that may be hanging

SIMPLE POTPOURRI

Either buy some plain potpourri mixture or make it up from dried flowers and woods that you like, but make sure it includes oak shavings, and, ideally, some thistles. Add five drops of citronella, geranium, and peppermint essential oils in a deosil (clockwise) motion. Repeat when the smell wears off. This will protect your home and those who live in it.

around the house. Then, bless the house by asking the spirits of the land and your ancestors to look after it and all who live in it.

☆☆☆

✪✪ Mice are cute, but you probably don't want them inside your home! This spell will help to remove them, and stop a new colony taking up residence.

Place a few pieces of smelly cheese where you have seen the mice, or suspect they may be. Think about how annoying the mice are, and how it would be better not just for you, but also for them to be outside.

Then, go to pick up the pieces of cheese, saying the following as you do so:
"Mice are nice,
but not in here.
I do not want them near!"

Go outside and walk away from your home with the cheese, and place it somewhere where you wouldn't mind the mice living, such as the bottom of the yard or under a nearby hedgerow.

This spell is best done on a waning moon, so as the moon diminishes in the sky, so does your mouse problem.

☆☆☆

✪ Cleanse the house spiritually by ringing a bell all around your home, especially in the corners of each room. Then bless the home by sprinkling rose water all around. Wash the windows with it if you like.

To cleanse and bless your home

✪ To remove the bad energies of past occupants and any negative history, first thoroughly clean the house with a vinegar-in-water solution; wash windows and floors, wooden or tiled, and sprinkle more on the walls. Secondly, ring a clear, high-pitched bell all around the house (see left).

☆ ☆ ☆

✪✪ To ward off hostile people, keep a broomstick by your front door; you can decorate it with protective sigils, for example squares, in blue. Lay it across the threshold when you are unsure of someone, and ask that person to step across it. Many negative people will refuse, but if he or she does walk across it, the broomstick will absorb some of the bad energy.

☆ ☆ ☆

✪✪ To attract the guardianship of the deities, light some sandalwood incense, and sprinkle some rose water around the home, especially in the corners and on things you use often, such as the bed and TV. If you cannot find rose water, you can make your own by adding a few drops of rose essential oil or some dried fragrant, rose petals to a small bottle of mineral water.

Write your own blessing to say as you walk around the home, something like:

"I bless this house so that it may become our true home, so we may have peace in it and feel safe and so we are always happy to return here. In the name of the Hearth Goddess, Brigit, I bless this home!"

To sell your home and find a new one

✪ Each morning at dawn (if possible), look at your house's listing on the internet, or at a paper copy if you have one, and chant:

"Quickly the house will be selling,
Solid new buyers today will bring
Money enough for me to retire,
So my situation is no longer dire!"

☆ ☆ ☆

✪ If a high price for your house is more important to you than a quick sale, burn some frankincense shortly before viewings. While you are tidying up in preparation for viewings, and burning the incense, imagine the prospective buyer smiling and handing over bundles of notes to you. Good luck!

☆ ☆ ☆

✪ To attract attention to your "for sale" sign, place a clear quartz crystal point behind it, by the street. Painting your front door a dark green—for prosperity—will help the house fetch a good price, but if this is not possible, keep a dark green plant with an oval leaf, such as a laurel bush, near the front door.

☆ ☆ ☆

✪✪ To help find the place where you should be living, get an old key. It should not be from your own home. In fact, it's best that you do not know what it is for—maybe get one from a secondhand store, or from a friend. Once a week at dusk, hold the key between your flat palms, close your eyes, relax, and slow your breathing. For a few minutes, think about your ideal home. With time, your thoughts will solidify into a concrete list of requirements and/or a definite area where you want to live.

☆ ☆ ☆

✪✪ To help decide where to live, when the moon is new, take a piece of blue paper and, with a white pen, write five reasons for moving there; then, with a black pen, write on the reverse side of the paper five reasons for not moving there. Repeat for each place under consideration. Place the papers under your pillow and read them each night before going to bed. By the Full Moon, you will have dreams guiding you to the right place.

☆ ☆ ☆

✿✿ To help you with a house move, get a carnelian stone, either a pebble or as part of jewelry. Once a week, while touching the stone, close your eyes for a few minutes, relax, and slow your breathing. Imagine yourself in your new home, happy and healthy. Carry your carnelian with you whenever you do anything related to the move.

☆☆☆

✿✿ On a piece of plain white paper, draw a square with a triangle on top on it—a very simple house. At the top of the square, on the left side, write the three things that are most important to you in a house.

If you have a partner, he or she should do the same thing at the bottom of the square on the right side, so that your paper house includes the most important things for both of you. In the middle of the square, draw a heart to symbolize the two of you being happy in your new home. Fold the paper four times—each of you twice in turn—and carry it with you whenever you go to look at houses or to meet agents.

☆☆☆

✿✿✿ Collect some water from the general area where you want to live, preferably from a natural source, such as a pond or river.

Light a beeswax candle (because it is made from the home of bees) in your cauldron and add the water gently so that the candle flame is an inch or two above the water. While you add the water, think about how the new home will water your creativity and ability to do what you like most.

Sit comfortably in front of this arrangement and slow your breathing. Gaze into the water and watch the candle flame's image dance on it. After a while, images should appear to you on the water surface; for example, you might see the candle flame shaped like a letter, which would mean you should look for a new home in a street starting with that letter, or you might see an identifiable shape.

If it is a bird, for example, that would mean you should look for a new home in a street named after a bird.

RELIABLE TENANT

To help you attract a suitable lodger, or someone dependable to rent your home to, when you first write your ad, do so with a green pen (to find prosperity through the rental) on yellow paper (for finding a friendly renter). When someone comes to view, place a clear crystal wrapped in a yellow cloth in the main room—hide it if you like, maybe in a plant pot—so the place will feel friendly and have strong, positive energy.

Friends and relatives

Useful ingredients

Some basic ingredients are good to have on hand in case you need to perform some nonlover relationship magic. I would recommend:

YELLOW ITEMS—this is the color of friendship, so keep some yellow paper and pens for writing "snail-mail" letters, and yellow ribbons or candles for spells.

BEESWAX CANDLES— beeswax is naturally yellow, and the work of the bees in creating the wax reminds you that even though a relationship sometimes takes hard work, the outcome is beautiful.

YELLOW FOODS—yellow bell peppers, squashes, and bananas enhance friendships. Use them as altar decorations while performing family and friendship spells, and serve dishes containing yellow ingredients at parties. As well as promoting friendship, these will bring the energy of the sun to you.

CARNELIAN GEMSTONE— the yellow-brown color of carnelian symbolizes friendship and its nurturing aspect. Brown is for Mother Earth.

GERANIUM AND PEPPERMINT— these are two great herbs for removing negativity and any petty annoyances that may have built up in a family relationship or friendship. They are easiest to use as essential oils on candles, in baths, or on cloth, but you can also serve peppermint tea or give potted herbs as gifts.

WHITE CLOTHING AND CANDLES— white is for pure, positive energy, and also for peace. If there are problems with members of your family, wear something white the next time you meet, or use white cloth to make a charm bag, or burn a few white candles.

To nurture and repair friendship

✪ Find two pieces of yellow carnelian that look very similar. Place them to the left of your bed to guide your intuition toward whether a friendship is worth the effort you are putting in.

☆☆☆

✪ To stop a neighbor or acquaintance draining your energy before he or she visits, imagine yourself standing in a bubble of yellow energy. Outside the bubble, there is a clean white sponge that soaks up any negative energy or neediness you cannot deal with.

After the person leaves, imagine the now dirty sponge falling away from you and being absorbed back into Mother Earth.

☆☆☆

✪ Take a long slip of paper (the till receipt from the last time you spent money on the dependent friend is ideal), and write your name on one end and your friend's name on the other end. Throw the piece of paper in the fire so it can burn away the negativity in this relationship.

☆☆☆

✪ If you are acquainted with someone whom you'd like to become a friend, write the name on white paper with a yellow pen and make a pentagram with five vanilla pods around it.

☆☆☆

✪ To make friends, light a yellow candle in the north part of your home—north is the Earth's element, which is nurturing, like a good friendship—and say:

"Friendship come to me,
Social anxieties, let me be!
I will have fun,
No longer back home I'll run."

Do this a couple of times a week for as long as necessary.

☆☆☆

✪✪ Rub geranium oil on a yellow candle to remove any obstacles to your talking

MAGIC ELIXIR

Pour hot water into a large mug and add a teaspoon of dried white
oak bark (for strength), three fresh mint leaves (to foster good relationships), and a
teaspoon of lemon zest (to encourage friendship and symbolize the Sun God);
add some honey to taste. This drink will give you inner strength. Share it with a friend,
or with someone you'd like to be more than a friend.

freely—yellow is for friendship and communication. Then, scratch your friend's name in the candle with a pin, or your athame (magical knife) if you have one. Light the candle and stand it near the phone, or your computer, for ten minutes twice a day. Communication should slowly increase. Light the candle more often if you are especially desperate to hear from them.

☆ ☆ ☆

✪✪ To help make new friends at a party, sports club, or other gathering, select something yellow to wear. This need not be visible; underwear or socks would be fine.

As you put on the yellow garment, say:
"Sometimes I am too meek,
But today friendship I seek.
I am looking for support and fun,
And now this spell is done!"

☆ ☆ ☆

✪✪ Make nine knots in a yellow ribbon, or a piece of string, that is 23cm (9in) long. Each time you tie a knot, chant:
"By the power of three times three, new
friendships I'll see!"

Carry the knotted ribbon or string with you wherever you go.

⚘ · TIP · ⚘

To attract new friends into your life, wear jewelry
made from lapis-lazuli or tiger's eye. This also helps
with work and business success.

To take care of family

✪ When children have nightmares, or are afraid of the dark, have them sprinkle rosemary around an area of their room that they can regard as their "safe zone." This will help to prevent nightmares, keep the room peaceful and help them to sleep better. Do it for children if you prefer them not to know about magic.

☆☆☆

✪ Here's a spell to try if some family members refuse to see your point of view. Next time they visit, brew some peppermint tea, add a spoonful of honey to each cup, and stir deosil (clockwise), chanting (under your breath if they are near):

"My family are difficult to take,
They are no piece of cake.
Please let them see
How difficult it is for me!"

☆☆☆

✪ If you are estranged from a member of your family because of some wrong you feel has been done to you, write that person a long letter on blue paper—blue for healing and wisdom—explaining why you are upset, but also saying that you don't want any bad feeling between you to continue.

Seal it in a white envelope—white for positive energy—if possible, adding a photo of the two of you happy together.

Address the envelope with a yellow pen—yellow for friendship.

Do not mail this letter, but keep it somewhere safe until the relationship is mended.

☆☆☆

✪ To find a family member with whom you have lost touch, or information about an ancestor, write that person's family tree, as far as you know it, up to three steps removed, that is up to great-grandparents and/or great-grandchildren.

Have the lost one's name in the center and use a green pen for prosperity and good luck. Then place a clear quartz crystal on the name to draw energy to it.

☆☆☆

✪ Empower white candy by leaving it out on the windowsill, wrapped, during a waxing moon.

The Moon Goddess will bless it with acceptance and love. Then offer the candy to your family when you visit.

Peppermint is good because it calms nerves and eases difficult relationships, and white is for peace. Have some yourself to clear negative emotions that may have built up over the years.

☆☆☆

79

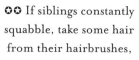

✪✪ If siblings constantly squabble, take some hair from their hairbrushes, bind it all together with blue ribbon—blue for peace and wisdom—and leave it in a place where they usually get on well, for example by the TV if they like the same shows.

☆ ☆ ☆

✪✪ This spell is to help children of divorced parents to cope with the situation.

Light a purple and a blue candle in front of a photo of your smiling kids—purple for insight and wisdom, blue for healing and calm. Gaze at the photo and visualize how they will be happy and well adjusted in the future. You can even say your plans for them out loud if you like. As you blow out the candles, say:

"Happiness and fun I seek for [your children's names]. *No longer angry they'll be, the truth of everything they'll see."*

Do this once every waxing moon to increase the children's understanding of the situation, and once every waning moon to reduce their anger, until you feel it is no longer necessary. Do it at other times, too, if they seem particularly upset.

☆ ☆ ☆

✪✪✪ When you are worried about a relative but don't want to be overprotective, or meddling, close your eyes, breathe deeply three times, and visualize the subject of your anxiety happy and laughing. Imagine that person picking up a phone and ringing you; watch him or her pressing each of the numbers, then putting the phone to his or her ear, and imagine your phone ringing. Soon, your phone will ring for real and your relative will tell you all is well.

DREAMS OF THOSE DEPARTED

Before bed, soak in a warm bath with geranium oil, then put on your favorite T-shirt, and go to sleep remembering good times with your departed loved one. Then, your dreams will be happy, and you will wake up feeling rested.

To look after your pet

✪ Make a simple drawing of the animal you'd like for a pet, using a blue pen, and place a suitable food item on top of it, such as catnip for a cat, a bone for a dog, or a carrot for a rabbit. Place this on your altar or windowsill with a request to the Goddess Bast to bring the right animal to you. When you find it, feed your new pet the spell food.

☆ ☆ ☆

✪ To discourage runaways, with your left index finger gently trace the shape of a Brigid's Cross (one with equal length "arms") on your pet's head, back, belly, and legs, each time saying:

"You will no longer roam, you will stay at home!"

This is best done when the moon is full, and can be repeated monthly to keep up the spell's strength.

☆ ☆ ☆

✪ To keep tiny, irritating insects away from your dog, add a few drops of geranium essential oil to the last rinse when you bathe him or her, or rub the oil into his or her neck while chanting nine times:

"Worms, ticks, and fleas,
Little critters no one sees,
Go away now, stay away.
Illness and annoyance, keep at bay!"

☆ ☆ ☆

✪✪ Protect your pet from harm by placing a photo of it on a blue cloth, and chanting the following lines:

"Goddess Diana, keeper of pets
Keep my [pet's name] safe till the sun sets
Please keep him/her out of harm's way
by his/her side, protectively stay!"

☆ ☆ ☆

✪✪✪ Here is a magical spell to help find a lost pet. Put a photo of the animal or something belonging to it, such as a toy or a collar, on a nice plate.

Sprinkle sugar in a deosil (clockwise) direction around the edge of the plate and explain to the faeries and spirits how important your animal companion is and why you would like him or her back. Slow your breathing, close your eyes, and mentally call your pet; you may have a flash of inspiration where he or she may be. If not, take the toy between your palms and visualize your animal friend coming through the door and being happy to see you.

Do this every day until your pet is found. Then gather all the sugar you used in the daily spells and sprinkle it on a faerie fort (a small hill where faeries are said to live) or into a fast-moving stream, giving thanks to the unseen powers that helped you find your much-loved pet.

CHAPTER 7

Health Spells

Health magic is a great way to complement alternative
and Western medicine. However, as with any magic, doing a
spell will not make the outcome certain, so consult your doctor about
ailments and illnesses, and ensure that performing a spell will not
interfere with any prescribed treatment; for example, some
herbs are contra-indicated with blood thinners or contraception.
Do not trust so-called witches who say they can cure you with magic
for a price. If someone doesn't approve of magic, don't perform
spells on their behalf, but you can still pray for them
to your own gods or angels.

In this chapter you will find
spells to help you:
⬦ reduce stress and build confidence
⬦ cope with illness and injury
⬦ with fertility and pregnancy
⬦ look after yourself

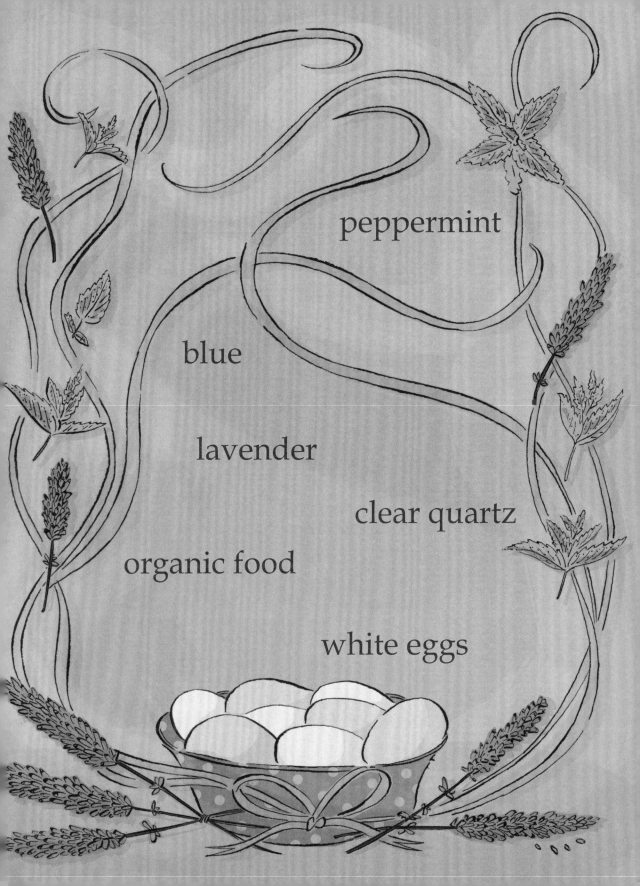

peppermint

blue

lavender

clear quartz

organic food

white eggs

Useful ingredients

Some basic ingredients are always good to have on hand in case you may need to perform some health magic. I would recommend:

BLUE ITEMS—blue is the color of healing and wisdom, and used in much health magic. Keep blue ribbons and scraps of blue cloth, and have some blue clothing ready in case you need it for yourself!

PEPPERMINT—a great cleanser and calmer, peppermint can be used in potpourri, as tea, or in magical foods. It is very easy to grow but can take over your garden.

LAVENDER—the ultimate stress-buster and calmer, this herb keeps for a long time in dried form, and makes everything smell nice, too.

CLEAR QUARTZ—a powerful gem for any magic, clear quartz is great to draw positive attention to you, bolstering your confidence and giving extra energy when you are tired or feeling low, or when you are recuperating after an illness.

WHITE EGGS—white stands for pure energy; the egg is a symbol of fertility, the blessing of the Mother Goddess, and the circle of life. It reminds us that being laid low with an illness helps us to appreciate our overall health.

FRESH, ORGANIC FOOD—magical recipes feature the color and shape of food. For example, red is for vigour, and green, phallic shapes are to encourage fertility. Thin vegetables are for losing weight.

To reduce stress and build confidence

✪ To help you cope with stress, and to remove the negativity and aggression of others toward you, add a spoonful of honey to fresh peppermint or camomile tea and stir in a deosil (clockwise) direction while chanting:

> *"Stress be gone!*
> *Negativity I want none.*
> *Friendliness and love shall bloom*
> *Brightness rules my day, not gloom!"*

Do this regularly and walk around with your tea, so others can smell it. Offer them some, too.

☆ ☆ ☆

✪ For inner strength and confidence, say the following while stirring food deosil (clockwise):

> *"Change I seek, no longer will I be meek!"*

☆ ☆ ☆

✪ Wear a clear quartz crystal against your skin at the level of your throat chakra to improve your confidence. Whenever you feel particularly anxious or unsure about having made the right choice, touch the quartz and say (under your breath when in public):

> *"I am strong, I am not wrong, the powers that be, guide my soul, my body, guide me."*

☆ ☆ ☆

✪ After a stressful day, before bed make a small cup of warm milk with honey. The whiteness of the milk stands for peace and calm, as well as the protection of the Moon Goddess, and honey represents the sweetness of a good night's sleep. Stir deosil (clockwise) and say:

> *"Sleep now come,*
> *Heaven it is from.*
> *May I sleep long and well*
> *Until the morning alarm bell!"*

To do this spell for a child, simply substitute the child's name for "I".

☆ ☆ ☆

✪ Find a square of blue cloth, such as a handkerchief, and on it draw an animal you associate with strength and endurance. It could be a bear, an eagle, a puma, or any other creature you choose.

Add a drop of lavender essential oil to each corner of the cloth, fold it four times and put it in your pocket or purse, carrying it with you at all times.

Replenish the lavender about once a week. Whenever you feel anxious or otherwise unwell, take out the cloth and unfold it slowly while breathing calmly through your nose.

☆ ☆ ☆

✪ After a traumatic event, such as a relationship break-up or physical attack, drop a small, rose quartz pebble in your cup every time you make tea, to help you relax and forget.

✩ ✩ ✩

✪✪ Comfort yourself by soaking in a stress-buster bath. Gather some lemon geranium or citronella to clear stress, cloves to absorb bad luck, camomile to calm the nerves, and cinnamon for love. Put the herbs in some white muslin—white for peace—and tie the corners together to make a ball. Add this to a warm bath, or hang it from the showerhead. When you are done with your bath, watch the water draining away and imagine all your stress disappearing with it.

✩ ✩ ✩

✪✪ To stop bad dreams and nightmares, sprinkle some dried rosemary around your bed in a protective circle, using a widdershins (counterclockwise) motion, while visualizing yourself sleeping deeply with a contented smile on your face. As you scatter the herb, chant the following:

*"Peaceful and calm will be my sleep
No bother, no nightmares—just calm and deep.
Soon, at work rewards I'll reap."*

It may also help to write down any specific problems you have before you go to bed, to get them out of your head, leaving your mind worry-free.

✩ ✩ ✩

✪✪ To boost self-esteem, put a statue of any strong animal you particularly like, such as a bear or an eagle, where it can catch the sun's rays, and visualize the sun and the spirit of the animal making you happy and strong. The statue doesn't have to be expensive; a plastic toy will do.

✩ ✩ ✩

🕯 · TIPS · 🕯

When feeling low, make some camomile or peppermint tea to calm the stomach and mind, and to stimulate your energy. Stirring food deosil (clockwise) with a red spoon, and eating from a red plate, will give you vigour and energy.

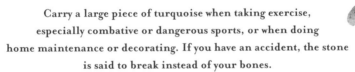

✪✪ Leave a closed pot of your favorite foundation cream or moisturizer in the light of a full moon overnight. As you place it in the window in the evening and take it back in the morning, pray for the love and guidance of the Maiden, Mother, or Crone Goddess corresponding to your age. Then, leave the pot in sunlight for a day, praying to the Sun God for energy, strength, and confidence as you place it in a constantly sunny spot in the early morning and remove it at dusk. You now have face cream that will lend you its positive, magical energy, giving you self-confidence whenever you find ourself with new people or in awkward social situations.

To cope with illness and injury

TURQUOISE FOR PROTECTION

Carry a large piece of turquoise when taking exercise, especially combative or dangerous sports, or when doing home maintenance or decorating. If you have an accident, the stone is said to break instead of your bones.

✪✪ To help ease someone's pain, carve his or her name in a blue candle and rub it with peppermint oil. Light the candle at least once a week, and also when you sense a weather change or that the person is in trouble, chanting the following five times:

"Discomfort and pain
All will now drain.
Lord and Lady I ask you undo
The pain and hurt [name] is going through."

☆ ☆ ☆

✪✪ To maintain wellness, in the morning before you get out of bed, visualize yourself in a blue bubble of healthy energy. Do the same for each of your children and other family members. Repeat whenever you feel anxious about health issues.

☆ ☆ ☆

✪✪ Lemon balm can be used to encourage a wound to heal quickly. Wrap a leaf of it around your athame if you have one, or otherwise a letter opener or blunt knife, and secure with blue string—blue for healing. Touch the wound lightly with the wrapped knife, asking the body's energy and Mother Nature to help with the healing. Lemon balm can easily be grown in a pot or in the garden, and it also makes great tea.

✩ ✩ ✩

✪✪ This spell helps to reduce discomfort. Gently wrap a photo of the person who is suffering in a piece of organic cotton— noncolored or white is best, but blue for healing would work, too—while chanting the following spell:

"I wrap you in cotton, I bind you with love, Protection from pain surrounds like a glove. May the brightest of blessings surround you this night, For you are cared for, pain is set to flight."

✪✪ To encourage fertility (see more on fertility, below), eat an egg daily from when you start a period to ovulation. As you eat, visualize your eggs growing and getting ready for fertilization. A man should eat a carrot daily; they stand for virility and are a potent phallic symbol.

To concentrate on fertility and pregnancy

✪✪ This spell to help you conceive is worth the effort of finding the main ingredient—the shed skin from a snake.

A zoo, animal shelter, or pet store may be able to help. Keep it in a green cloth under the bed. The skin symbolizes renewal and growing babies, and green represents fertility and a positive future.

✩ ✩ ✩

✪✪ For a healthy pregnancy, take a perfect apple or pear, one with no blemishes, cuts, or other marks. Choose an apple if you are hoping for, or know, the baby is a boy, and a pear for a girl.

While praying to Cerridwen, Freya, or Brigit, or another Mother Goddess, for a healthy pregnancy, rub the fruit

clockwise over your belly. Then, cut it in as many pieces as you have months left before the birth, and bury the pieces in fertile soil. You can repeat this spell once a month throughout your pregnancy, if you like.

✩ ✩ ✩

✪ On a red candle, inscribe the name you are considering for your baby—it's okay to change your mind later. Tie a blue ribbon around the candle for healing and calm, and to avoid getting stressed, and a green one for fertility. Place the lighted candle on the bedside table whenever you are doing "the baby dance." Don't forget to blow the candle out afterwards.

✩ ✩ ✩

✪ You can perform this spell for a friend after a difficult delivery, or for yourself and your baby. Light a blue candle—for healing— in front of a photo of mother and child while chanting nine times:

"Hard was your coming into this world
Difficulties abound as your life unfurled.
But now happiness and love will abound
Smiles and health all around!"

☆ ☆ ☆

✪✪ Here's a spell to help a stressed-out new mother to relax (although nothing works better than bringing around a homemade dinner and letting her sleep for a few hours while you do the housework!)

Write the names of mother and baby on white paper with a blue pen—white for peace, blue for calm and healing—and decorate the paper with violets. Dried or candied flowers are fine, or just draw them.

Violets stand for tranquility, loving energies, and acceptance. If the picture comes out well, you could give it to the new family as a gift.

WEAR CORAL

If long or painful periods are a problem, wear a bracelet of coral beads around your left wrist. The left is the female side of the body.

To look after yourself

✪ Write your name on a slim white candle with blue crayon—white for pure energy and a new start, blue for health. Light the candle first thing in the morning, before eating anything, and look into the flame and say:

"I need to lose the weight
So I'll have a healthier gait.
Lord and Lady guide me
Slim and happy I want to be!"

☆ ☆ ☆

✪ To stop eating unhealthy food, or simply eating too much, light a slim white candle before every meal and sugary snack, such as donuts, and visualize yourself healthy and happy. While you do this, you can also ask Sekhmet, the goddess of healing and beauty, for help with a simple chant, such as:

"Sekhmet I ask thee, make me realize
I am pretty!"

☆ ☆ ☆

✪ Try a magical oatmeal body and face scrub to help you feel heavenly. Add some honey to oatmeal, stirring in a deosil (clockwise) direction while chanting the following nine times:

"I am beautiful, I am divine. Health and happiness will be mine!"

Then rub the concoction deosil (clockwise) into your skin.

☆ ☆ ☆

✪✪ To attract the divine allure of the goddess Venus, buy some sparkly silver powder and, at dawn, look up at the morning star, thinking about the things you find beautiful about yourself, inside and out.

With both hands, hold the sparkly powder up toward the morning star and, in your own words, ask Venus to take away your imperfections, and let everyone see your most gorgeous side, your inner goddess.

Apply the powder in a heart shape on your chest and anywhere else you wish for some enhancement of your natural beauty, for example your legs if you feel they could be more shapely, or your hair if you don't like it.

You can disperse the powder afterward, or cover it up with clothes.

☆ ☆ ☆

✪✪ This spell helps to get rid of an addiction. Do it every dawn and dusk, or as close to those times as possible, and also when you feel the craving kicking in.

Touch your chest with your right thumb, middle, and ring finger while the other two fingers are stretched away from the body.

Take three deep breaths, imagining the physical and mental signs of the addiction leaving your body.

For example, for a smoking habit, think of the black tar coming out of your lungs with each breath.

BEAUTIFUL OATS

A handful of oats in the bath will soften your skin and will also bring you closer to the Moon Goddess, to whom oats are sacred. Start any beauty routine focusing on improvement on a waxing moon, so your success will correspond to the increase in the moon's size; and start any program to lessen imperfections or lose weight on a waning moon, so the problems will decrease in the same way.

Say:

"This addiction, this need
I want it gone with speed!
I call it gone, I speak it gone, I declare
it gone!"

This spell won't work immediately, but it will lead to a gradual decrease of whatever addiction plagues you.

☆ ☆ ☆

⊙⊙ To help your doctor or consultant to find the right diagnosis and treatment for your ailment, write his or her name in green, for prosperity and a good future, and cover it with purple cloth.

The purple is for knowledge. If you can find a photo of the doctor on the hospital's website, print that and put it in the cloth, too. Place this by a statue of an owl, or on a picture of an owl, to help guide the doctor in wisdom.

☆ ☆ ☆

⊙⊙ Warts and verrucas can be a nuisance. A spell to help get rid of them involves a potato with "eyes"—if you leave a potato out in daylight for a week or so, eyes will develop. When the moon is waning, cut the potato in half, then rub one cut side widdershins (counterclockwise) on your warts or verrucas. Place the two halves of the potato back together and bury it in the earth where you can walk over it every day, such as in your front yard.

As the potato disintegrates and vanishes back into Mother Earth, so your warts or verrucas will disappear.

☆ ☆ ☆

⊙⊙ For insomnia, drink a cup of vervain or camomile tea each evening, about thirty minutes before you go to bed.

Add a spoonful of honey, first stirring widdershins (counter-clockwise) while you imagine all the worries and stress of the day leaving you, then deosil (clockwise) as you think of a good night's sleep and the positive things that are going to happen tomorrow.

☆ ☆ ☆

⊙⊙⊙ This spell will help you to overcome the last of an eating disorder, in conjunction with conventional treatment from your doctor and counsellor. Make a strong infusion with vervain and/or lemon balm, pour some into a cup and drop a clear quartz crystal into it. Swirl around gently widdershins (counterclockwise) while saying:

"Eating disorders stay away from me.
Get away, leave me be!"

Then swirl deosil (clockwise) and say:

"I will stay healthy and strong as surely as the
day is long!"

Take the clear quartz out and keep it in your pocket as a health talisman.

CHAPTER 8

Other Spells

This chapter contains an array of spells that didn't
fit into any of the other chapters. I wanted to include them
because they are useful, proven successful, and on topics
I am asked about regularly, especially happiness and contentment,
but also other, smaller issues—even finding a parking space!
They prove that there is magic for almost everything, and
spells don't have to be overly serious—laughter and fun can
enhance the positive energy in magic.

Useful ingredients

Some basic ingredients are always good to have on hand in case you may
need to perform some general magic. I would recommend:

WHITE CANDLES—when all else fails,
white candles represent pure energy and
can boost the power of any spell, or
represent other colors.

CLEAR QUARTZ
CRYSTAL—the "white
candle" of the gem world,
clear quartz crystals are beacons
of energy and will draw positive attention to
the wearer or object with which they are
kept. Commonly used as crystal points, that
is having a jagged or peaked end, they can

also be utilized as clear pebbles for a
smoother, more harmonious energy.

PURPLE—this color stands for occult
knowledge, so burning a purple candle
during the writing and/or performing
of a spell can help you gain
insight and make sure the
spell is done correctly.

REAWAKEN YOUR FEMALE ENERGY

✪ To reconnect with your female energy—for example when having irregular periods, or working in an all-male office, or similar—make sure you have some time to yourself, ideally on Mondays, the day of the Moon Goddess. This will help you to feel feminine and strong again. Watch a girly movie and drink some hot milk with honey.

✪ To make a decision between three different paths, on a New Moon, take three pieces of paper. With a blue pen, write on each one five positive things about taking that path and on the other side, with a black pen, write down five negative things about that path. Fold each paper three times while saying:

*"God and Goddess guide me,
my true path let me see!"*

Put the papers away until the Full Moon, then read again and make your decision.

✪ To protect things from getting lost, sprinkle fairy dust near the items you want to protect. Fairy dust is a mixture of anything small and sparkly such as little gold stars and glitter. The fairies will be attracted to this instead of your items. For example, on my bedside table, I have a small blue velvet box full of fairy dust, always open. I keep my jewelry, bank cards, and other valuable items in the drawers of this table and have never lost one of them!

✪ To find a parking space, have a piece of chocolate in your car; when in need of a parking space, chant the following:

"Parking fairy I am in a bind, but a parking space I will find!"

Once you have parked, drop the chocolate by the curb with thanks to the fairy.

✪ To prevent your bike being stolen, and to avoid accidents, rub it with a clove, while saying:

*"Hermes, God of Travellers,
I ask thee
To protect and keep safe my bike and me;
To transport us and have fun,
My healthy life has begun!"*

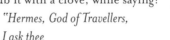

✪ To unblock your creativity, make sure you have some time to yourself at least twice a week, even if it is just a nice long bath. Before this time, hold a clear crystal to your forehead to activate your third eye and to give yourself creative energy to think.

✪ This is a simple winter spell to help you accept change in your life, whether that's good, such as moving in with your partner or a promotion; or bad, such as losing a job or breaking up with your partner. Find a piece of ice shaped like a wand—an icicle from outside your home is best. Face North, and draw a pentagram in the air with your ice wand, saying:

"Ice to earth, give me strength!"

Then turn East, draw a pentagram again while saying:

"Ice to air, give me inspiration!"

Turn South and repeat, saying:
"Ice to fire, give me passion!"

and lastly turn West, draw another pentagram and say:

"Ice to water, help me weather this change!"

Hold the ice wand to your forehead, mouth and heart, and then place it outside so it may re-freeze or melt.

☆ ☆ ☆

✪✪ If there is something you want to keep secret, find something that symbolizes it, such as a photo of you and your love if you want to keep the relationship secret. Place it between the top and bottom part of a crabshell, and keep this somewhere safe.

☆ ☆ ☆

✪✪ To make a charm bag for protection, in a yellow cloth place a turquoise stone and a whole nutmeg. The yellow is for alertness and memory, the turquoise stone is to prevent injury, and the nutmeg is to remove negativity and attract good luck. Sprinkle with a pinch of cumin for protection and preventing bad luck, and with black pepper to keep negative situations and people away. Tie the bundle with purple string or ribbon. Purple is primarily for occult knowledge, but also pre-cognition, and "forewarned is forearmed"!

☆ ☆ ☆

✪✪ If you have mislaid jewelry or a cherished heirloom, place a photo or drawing of the lost item on a pretty plate. Sprinkle sugar in a deosil (clockwise) circle on the edge of the plate, and explain to the fairies how important the piece is to you and why you need it back. Close your eyes and slow your breathing; you will feel drawn to the place where the item is. If you find it, thank the fairies by sprinkling some sugar on the plate every day for a week.

☆ ☆ ☆

✪✪ To remind you of the good things in life, each morning look at a happy personal picture that relates to the power of that day. Monday is for motherhood and family, so look at a photo of you with your extended family; Tuesday is for new

If you need more self-confidence to carry out a plan, lightly touch your closed eyelids with a tiger's eye before you need to act.

beginnings and changes, so look at a drawing of your wedding ring; Wednesday is for communication and getting rid of fear, so look at a photo of yourself laughing with a friend; Thursday is for money and debt, so look at a picture of coins and notes; Friday is for love, so look at a photo of you with your partner; Saturday is for getting rid of negativity and freedom, so look at a photo of yourself on holiday; Sunday is for success and healing, so if, for example, you are selling your home, look at a photo of you happy in front of the "for sale" sign.

☆☆☆

✪✪ If you need to travel during bad weather, take a small square of blue cloth. If you have any particular deities or angels you like, call on them. On the cloth, place three cloves, saying:

"I ask you to keep away negativity and bad luck!"

Then add five peppercorns and say:

"I ask you to protect me/us from adversity in this weather!"

Add some ginger and say:

"I ask you to bless me/us with warmth and health!"

Lastly, add some coarse salt and say:

"I ask you to keep away harm from water in all forms and bring the blessings and protection of Mother Earth!"

Fold the cloth to contain all the ingredients and tie it shut with a white ribbon—white for energy and peace. Carry this with you on your travels. Make another one for the car. If you do this spell for someone who is traveling to visit you, include a photo of them, or their name written on white paper in blue pen, and keep the bundle somewhere safe and warm until they arrive.

☆☆☆

✪✪✪ To feel more love for yourself, perform this spell on a Monday if you are a woman, Sunday for a man. Take a piece of white paper. With a blue pen, write down three things you'd like to change about yourself; with a yellow pen, write down six things you like about yourself; and with a green pen, write down nine things that others have said are good about you. It may take time, but you will find nine things! Fold the paper three times—once to remove negativity, once to remind yourself of your blessings, and once to invite love into your life. Read the paper whenever you feel low.

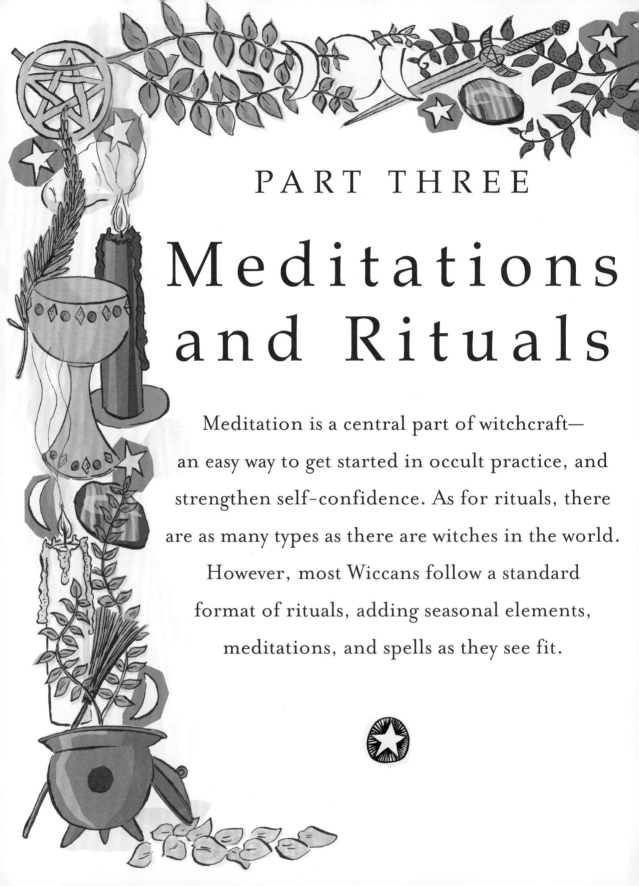

PART THREE

Meditations and Rituals

Meditation is a central part of witchcraft—
an easy way to get started in occult practice, and
strengthen self-confidence. As for rituals, there
are as many types as there are witches in the world.
However, most Wiccans follow a standard
format of rituals, adding seasonal elements,
meditations, and spells as they see fit.

Wiccans use meditation for many purposes, from raising energy for a ritual or spell to calming the mind before divination, and simply for spiritual exercise and concentrating on specific tasks. It is a great tool for honing the intuition so important for witchcraft. Meditation is something that can be done in a minute or in an hour, and so reflects the immense adaptability inherent in Wicca.

Wiccans celebrate major life milestones, but have the flexibility of choosing what occasions to mark and how to do it. There are no rules: Wiccans devise their own rituals to celebrate more than life's three main events of birth, marriage, and death, by formally marking occasions such as pregnancy, puberty, menopause, and even divorce.

CHAPTER 9

About Meditations

Meditations are wonderful because they work well for
beginners and advanced witches alike, so an informal group
or a coven can meditate together, even though everyone has different
levels of experience. They are also easy, and effective, to do alone.
This chapter tells you all you need to know about
meditations, explaining the different types and how to prepare
yourself and your environment to be able to meditate successfully—
there is no need to sit in the lotus position for hours!

The following pages explain different types of
meditation and how to prepare for meditating.
There are sample ones for you to try,
including energy-raising meditations.

How to start a meditation

Set aside some quiet time just for yourself in a place
where you are not nervous about being interrupted and can
concentrate on relaxing. Choose something comfortable to wear.
Work-out clothes or a long, wide skirt are good, made from natural
cloth, such as cotton. Man-made fabric does not allow your skin
to breathe properly. Have a long soak in the bathtub
beforehand, and scent the water with some essential
oils, such as sandalwood or frankincense, that
promote a meditative state.

☦ · TIPS · ☦

Concentrate on relaxing and slowing down your breathing while holding an amethyst pebble against your forehead, in between and slightly above your eyes, for a few minutes. This is the location of your third eye and the procedure will help you get into your meditation.

There is no need for a quiet room and special clothes to meditate. If you are travelling by bus or train, watching the landscape pass by is a wonderful opportunity for a quiet meditation on Mother Nature.

Mythology is a great jumping-off point for meditation. Sit quietly gazing at a picture of a mythological story, and ask the deities depicted for inspiration on a vision quest, or the answer to a question you may have. Another way is to close your eyes and start telling yourself a mythological story. What would you have done differently from those in the original story, and why? Include yourself as a character. This will give you clues to solve current issues in your life and to reach your goals.

I also find that Buddhist-type mandalas can concentrate the mind and focus it inward before magical work, and help you to enter a trance for a guided meditation. Suitable mandala art need not be expensive. I often cut out drawings or photos from magazines and frame them, or buy coffee-table books by artists who inspire me. I then use a page a day to meditate over.

PRACTICE

Once you have found a procedure that's right for you and have done it a few times, you will find a meditative state will become easier to achieve. Then, you can use meditation to relax as opposed to having consciously to relax to meditate.

Types of meditation

CONCENTRATION

The easiest type of meditation is simply
to let go of stress and sit quietly and
comfortably, concentrating on relaxing
your body and focusing inward as opposed
to on outer negativity. This is a starting
point for most types of meditation.

VISUALIZATION

Simple visualizations are often involved in
spells. Close your eyes, or look into the
middle ground while letting your eyes
relax, and imagine whatever it is
you want to happen.
For example, you
may visualize
yourself and your
partner making
up after an
argument,
or an absent friend picking up the phone
to call you.

"HAPPY PLACE"

This technique builds on visualization and
can really help you to keep calm in stressful
situations and balanced when events trigger
an emotional response, be that anger or
sadness. Sit comfortably, or lie down, and
close your eyes. Now imagine your ideal
place, surrounded by nature. It may be
under a big tree on top of a hill, in the
middle of a cornfield, or on a sandy beach.

For me, it's in a forest glade with a babbling stream. Fill in all the details in your mind—hear the birds singing, feel the moss under your feet, smell the salty air from the sea. Spend several meditative sessions constructing your happy place, and once you are finished, practice going there in your mind whenever you have a free moment—while waiting in line somewhere or making a hot drink. Soon, you will be able to escape to your happy place easily, and you can go there for a moment of relaxation at any time, for example, before a business meeting, or when your three-year-old is being difficult.

GUIDED MEDITATION

Someone else does the talking in this type of meditation, and following the words makes it easier for you to achieve a deep meditative state. Plenty of guided meditation discs are available to buy or download, but many of them do not first explain the basics of relaxing, or they move into the actual meditation too quickly; so before playing them, make sure you are comfortable and fully relaxed, breathing slowly and deeply. Alternatively, you could get together with some friends, and one person could do the talking each week while the others meditate; or, if you are on your own, read a meditation into your computer and then play it back.

VISION QUEST

For this, you go deep into your subconcious to find out what to do about an issue, or to meet a deity or a spirit to help you with a goal in your life. This can be unsettling at first. I recommend that you practice the more basic forms of meditation until you are completely at ease with them, and hone your intuition as well as your knowledge of Wiccan spirituality, before going on a vision quest, which is an advanced form of meditation. In covens, vision quests are often undertaken as guided meditations, but that doesn't mean they are easy. Some examples of vision quests are given on pages 109–15.

GOOD PREPARATION

A pre-meditation bath helps to relax your mind and body and get you into a meditative state. You could add sandalwood to clear your mind, goat's milk to relax your muscles, and bergamot to deepen the meditative state.

Energy-raising meditations

To energize yourself, or charge a magical tool, you do not
necessarily have to sit comfortably and relax. After all, who wants
to sit like a Zen master when filled with positive energy?
These meditations can be done when you're feeling drained—for
example, during dreary winter months—or at the beginning of a
ritual to help with the magic. In that case, it is important to dispel any
remaining energy after the spell is complete, because otherwise it can
feel like you've had ten cups of espresso coffee on an
empty stomach!

Simple ways to raise energy

Environmental energy is dispelled by letting it sink into the
ground or storing it in magical tools and crystals.

Energy within you is dispelled by having something to eat
and drink—the "cakes and ale" part of a ritual—and placing your hands
palms down onto the ground or your altar, imagining all excess
energy leaving the body.

✪ Raising energy is usually a combination of mental and physical exercise. A simple way to do it is by drumming, slowly at first and then faster and faster. You can use kitchen pots and pans, or your desk or altar. Dancing around your magical circle is another easy way to raise energy, maybe to a witchy CD, or create your own dance inspired by a mythological story. Chanting a certain phrase, or sounds, over and over again also works well (see box, below).

SIMPLE CHANTS

These are effective in raising energy: "Ommmmmm", "Energy, come to me! Warm and active, I will be", "Eeeeh—ner—gyyyy."

✪ To energize yourself in the morning, before you open your eyes, take a few breaths and feel sleep leaving your body. Imagine lethargy sinking into the bed. Feel the rays of the sun warm your body and fill it with energy for the day ahead, even if the drapes are closed and the weather is overcast. When you open your eyes, you will be ready for the day.

☆ ☆ ☆

✪ Speak a prayer or simple visualization out loud. Saying the words tends to make them more "real," especially if you are new to energy-raising meditations, and also symbolically puts your request out there for the universe to act upon. Afterwards, spend a quiet minute or two to allow the energy to build up.

☆ ☆ ☆

A FULL MOON ENERGY-RAISING PRAYER

"This is the time of the Full Moon
When the moon-power is strong.
This is a time for all positive works
And so, as my patron spirits and deities are with me,
Allow me to gather my thoughts and my power,
My wishes and desires for the coming months,
and have the energy to fulfill them all!"

✪ For a more meditative way of raising energy, try standing with your feet hip-width apart, arms loosely by your sides. Close your eyes and imagine a stream of golden light piercing the top of your head and flowing down into all parts of your body. Feel it warming you. If you like, ask a specific deity to lend you some energy at this point. Then, imagine a similar stream of light entering your body through the soles of your feet, flowing up through your legs and all the way up into your head. Imagine the two streams mixing so that you are glowing, beaming like a beacon of energy and light.

☆ ☆ ☆

✪✪ To charge a crystal for a specific purpose, such as healing or love magic, place it on your altar and sit comfortably before it. Visualize pale pink or pale green light surrounding your receptive hand (your left if you are right-handed or vice-versa) and feel the warmth of the energy flowing up your arm and through your body into your projective hand (your right if you are right-handed.) Allow this to continue until you feel the time is right; then, using your projective hand, direct the energy toward the crystal, saying:

"With the blessing of the great Goddess,
Who breathes life into us all,
We consecrate and charge this crystal
As a magical tool for [insert purpose here.]"

☼ · TIP · ☼

If you do an energy-raising meditation in the open, visualize male energy from Father Sky entering through your head, and female energy from Mother Earth through your feet, providing perfect balance.

You can charge any magical tool, or jewelry, in the same way.

☆☆☆

✪✪ Imagine you are standing in a circle on the ground, and the circle is glowing with energy. Visualize it starting to rotate and slowly rise up all around you. Start turning around in a deosil (clockwise) direction. See the cone of energy encasing you, and when it does, close your eyes and stop spinning. It is good if you are a little dizzy, but you should not be woozy or stumble. Feel the warmth of the cone around you, its light and energy entering you. Then, feel the cone slowly sink into the ground, taking any excess energy with it. Open your eyes, full of energy and ready to do your spell or to go about your day.

☆☆☆

✪✪ Stand in front of a focal point, such as your altar or a single white candle. Close your eyes and ask your patron deities, ancestors, or spirit guides to help you.

Take in nine deep breaths, filling your lungs completely. With each breath, imagine the white light of pure, positive energy entering your body through your nose, filling your lungs and from spreading to the rest of your body.

Exhale through your mouth and imagine your problems and negative energy, thoughts, and emotions as black smoke leaving your body, being dispersed into the world where the spirits can recycle it into positive energy. Take nine more deep breaths, but this time, imagine all the pure energy staying within you, filling you from your abdominal core outward.

CHAPTER 10

Vision Quests and Visualizations

This chapter features a range of visualizations and vision quests.
They are a starting point to give you an idea of what is possible;
you can use them straight out of the book, or add your
own elements to them, such as seeking to talk to
your patron deity.

Once you feel comfortable with some of these simple to
slightly more intricate meditations, you may find that you
develop a special fondness for one or two. It is okay to do
them over and over again, and this can in fact help with getting
deeper into the meditative state. You can also lengthen
the visualizations and vision quests by combining some
elements from different meditations—and, of course,
as I always advocate, by adding your own parts.

Vision quest for Diana's guidance

To gain the goddess Diana's guidance and strength during difficult times for you, find an oak tree that you can stand under—an oak grove is ideal, but is not necessary.

Stand with your back against the sturdy trunk. Close your eyes and slow your breathing. Ask the goddess to lend you her resolve and her strength. Feel Diana's energy come through the roots of the oak, through its trunk, and flow into your body.

When you are filled with her energy, thank her, and ask for the blessing of a sign to indicate what you should do next. Open your eyes and look around.

If you see any flower, notice the color. For example, yellow means you should concentrate on friendships; red suggests you become more passionate about following your goals. Birds stand for artistic inspiration. If you see a woman of your own age walking past, this means that you should pay more attention to your female rather than your male friends.

Vision quest to find your magical name

Breathe deeply and relax your whole body. Ask your patron deities, or any gods and goddesses you especially like, to inspire you; you may see glimpses of them out of the corner of your eye, or feel a hand on your shoulder, or the room warming up.

Explain to the deities that you feel ready for your magical name, why you feel ready, and why you want one. Hold out your hands and ask the deities to lead you to the place where you can find your name; you may see only darkness for a while, or find your mind wandering through past events, or discover yourself flying high above the town where you live. Your journey could take some time; let it.

Eventually, you will see a spinning ball of light in the distance. Move toward it. You will not be able to look away because it is so beautiful and filled with positive magical energy. It gets bigger and bigger until it encases you in its brilliance and blinds you with light. The ball collapses and you are in complete darkness.

Just then, a word or symbol will appear, made from the brilliant light you saw

---

SPECIAL CHOICE

You can either do this vision quest without any preparation
to keep a completely open mind, or if you want to find a specific type
of name, for example that of an ancestor, or of a color or an animal,
first write down what you want your name to symbolize, such as inner
strength, compassion, or wisdom and so on.

---

before; it illuminates you and you realize you are no longer blind. This word or symbol is a hint of your name, or may be your name itself. Consider it carefully and take your time; it will become obvious, maybe so much so that you feel silly!

Thank the deities for their guidance and bid them farewell. As you feel them leave, become more aware of your physical surroundings and open your eyes.

Call your new magical name out loud five times; if your voice quivers or you feel strange doing so, reconsider the name.

Contact your totem animal or guardian angel

Sit or lie down comfortably. Close your eyes, breathe deeply and slowly relax all of your body, starting with your toes, then your feet, legs and so on until you are completely relaxed. Imagine yourself at the mouth of a deep cave. You walk into the cave and follow a spiraling path deep down into the earth. At the bottom, you see a small, dark pool of water. Look into the water, and you will see your guardian, whether as a name, a face, or an animal.

☊ · TIP · ☊

To train your powers of visualization, take a few minutes every day,
close your eyes and visualize what you saw just before you closed your eyes—for
example, your computer screen, a book, or your dinner.

A simple water meditation

Dress in blue or gray; eat some rice, tuna, or seaweed—the colors and foods that symbolize water.

Then, close your eyes and visualize a snake or a fish, or if you prefer, hold a sapphire—these are animals and the gem symbolizing water.

Pray to one of the water deities—Lir, Neptune, and Poseidon are water gods; Boann, Venelia, and Latis water goddesses. Wait until you can see the deity in front of you and have a real conversation. Let the deity guide you in emotional matters, especially if you have been sad lately, or unable to let go of emotional ties.

☼·TIP·☼

You can do the same type of simple vision quest for the other elements, too; see the chart on pages 136–7.

Dealing with disappointment or loss

Make your left hand into a fist, close your eyes, calm your breathing and visualize the Goddess Rhiannon, on a beautiful white horse, riding toward you.

Talk with her about your loss or disappointment. Be still, and she will dismount her horse and talk to you, or offer you another sign to help you—she might give you something.

Open your left hand and shake Rhiannon's hand; in this way, she will take all loss and disappointment from you.

Then, visualize her getting back onto her horse and riding away, taking your negative emotions with her. Open your eyes and go about your day. You can repeat this meditation whenever you feel it is necessary.

Vision quest to find answers

Sit comfortably, ideally cross-legged on the floor. Close your eyes and imagine yourself in a forest glade. Feel the slightly damp grass, smell the mushrooms and pine needles, notice a slight breeze. It feels warmer than it should in a forest, and as you look around, you see a small fire with a bubbling cauldron suspended over it.

You stand up to walk toward it, and as you do so, you see a magnificent stag. Your movement makes him notice you and he turns his head toward you, looking directly into your eyes. This is the god of the forest. He is strong and wise, and the guardian of all who live within the forest. You spend a long time looking into each other's eyes.

Listen to your mind and your body; he may give you a message this way.

After a while, the stag lowers his head slightly as if nodding and moves off. You walk to the cauldron and as you come closer, you notice many people sitting around it. Once you get close enough to see their faces lit up by the fire's flames, you see that these are all the people in your life, past and present, who have given you wise counsel.

There may be some companion animals, too, that have passed away. Sit with them and rest. Maybe one of them will approach you and give you something, or talk to you briefly. Think about what they say, but do not reply. They are here to talk to you, and for you to listen, not to chat.

An old woman, a figure you recognize as a wise crone, comes out from the darkness. She has an owl perched on her shoulder and wears a triple moon crown. The crone goddess goes to the cauldron and plunges a chalice into the hot, bubbling liquid, but it does not hurt her. She blows on the chalice to cool it, and as she does so, the owl flies from her shoulder and a feather from his wing drifts into the chalice. The goddess smiles and nods in approval of this omen. She then hands the chalice to you, motioning you to drink.

As you drink, the fog of uncertainty about your issue lifts, and answers come to you as if on the wings of an owl. You close your eyes and think upon the answers. When you open your eyes, the goddess and your companions are gone, and you are back in the room where you started.

☖ · TIP · ☖

If you find a feather within a day or two of doing this meditation, especially one still drifting in the wind, be sure to keep it and place it on your altar or bedside table. It will bring you even more inspiration and answers to your problem.

Mother Goddess nourishing vision quest

Sit or lie comfortably and place your palms on your lower abdomen (pregnant women should place their hands where the baby is). Inhale deeply nine times and, each time, visualize the yellow energy and power of the Sun God swirl around you, and the brown nourishing energy of the Mother Goddess coming up from the earth. Say:

"I am now receiving the blessing and protection of all Mother Goddesses, and all the mothers in my family line. May they protect and guide me!"

Visualize your mother and any other wise, nourishing women in your life, past and present, one by one. Greet them and ask them if they have any advice for you. Listen if they do! When you are done, exhale from deep within you nine times and visualize protective energies and blue light—blue for health and wisdom—coming out of you with each breath; visualize this light traveling to your children, if you have any, as well as other people and animals you take care of.

Flying vision quest for inspiration

Sit or lie comfortably, take some deep breaths, and relax your whole body. Feel yourself getting lighter and lighter, and lifting up into the air slightly; each deep breath takes you a little higher. Flex your fingers and your toes and visualize them sprouting feathers. Visualize moving them like strong wings, and flying out of the room. Soon, you are flying in the sky above your house, then higher up, into the clouds or into the night sky. You smile, enjoying the freedom and fun of flying. You notice birds flying around you, but also spirit creatures, such as fairies and maybe even angels.

You fly higher, and are warmed by the sun, feeling the blessing of the Sun God, or, if night time, the blessing of the Moon Goddess. You see people on the ground, rushing to and fro, and realize how small their problems really are, and yours, too. Everything can be solved with patience, love, and understanding, and maybe a little magic and hard work.

Sit upon a cloud, and take note of its shape; it may give you inspiration on where to go next in your spiritual learning, or how to approach a negative situation, or anything else about which you need inspiration. When you feel filled with happiness and contentment, hop off the cloud and slowly drift back to Earth, back into your room, and back into your body. Smile as you open your eyes, knowing you can always gain inspiration from the spiritual powers around you and your inner self.

Develop insight

This shapeshifting meditation helps you to train your powers of intuition, connect with a spirit animal, and see things from different points of view. Sit or lie down, relax, and slow your breathing. Close your eyes and imagine you are an animal. Feel your limbs changing, and your fur or feathers being ruffled by the wind. Visualize seeing your room from the animal's perspective—from above if you are a raven, from way below if you are a mouse, from a countertop if you are a goldfish. Then imagine "breaking free." In your mind, go outside. Saunter down the street as a cat; swim in a stream as a fish. Lastly, visualize your animal self in its natural habitat, before slowly returning your mind to your own body, and opening your eyes.

Find a new home

Every Sunday, which is the day for achieving goals, before you go to sleep, relax in bed and think about what you want from your future home—for example, the location, the number of bedrooms, the rent or mortgage you can afford. Then visualize a home that has these things. Pay attention to any dreams you have that night, because they could contain hints on how to acquire your ideal home.

Contact ancestors

If you wish to talk to your departed grandmother, or another loved one who has passed on, go to her grave or a place she loved and light a yellow candle, ideally while facing east. Think about her for a while, then speak a message out loud. Gently blow out the candle and watch the smoke disappear into the air, carrying your message to her.

LOOKING FOR LOVE

Visualization can help you find love, but never think of a specific person because this could impact on their free will. Simply imagine someone holding you lovingly from behind, so you can't see the face. If you are looking for marriage, see yourself with a partner at the altar or looking down at your entwined hands and wedding rings.

Remove a mental block

Start by sitting comfortably, closing you eyes, relaxing, and slowing down your breathing. Then, visualize yourself walking down a very long spiral staircase in almost complete darkness. At the bottom of the stairs is a stone path for you to follow. You find it difficult to see at first, but ask the beautiful Full Moon—the Mother Goddess—to guide you. Pay attention to what is on either side of the path; you may see animals that can help you as spirit guides in future meditations, or figures who look like ancestors or lost friends. Continue walking until you have found a clue to the next meditation, and/or what your mental block may be. Then, visualize being back at the spiral staircase. Climb up it and when you are at the top, slowly open your eyes. Take a few minutes to think about what you have seen in the meditation before moving.

Melt away trouble

Make yourself comfortable, relax, close your eyes. Visualize that you are on a faery fort (a small hill where elves and faeries are said to live), which is covered in snow. Slowly circle your way up it while thinking about a conundrum or an issue you are struggling with. When you reach the top, look down on the spiral made by your footprints. It is a breezy day and you have a flask of something warming with you—tea or mulled wine. Sip the warm drink while visualizing your troubles being carried away by the breeze, and inspiration to solve your issue being carried to you. Then, retrace your steps, slowly unwinding the spiral and thus unraveling any troubles that have slowed down your success so far. Gently open your eyes and readjust to your surroundings

---

☙ ·TIP· ☙

This visualization also works on a muddy hill, where you can see your footprints in the soil, or on a hill with long grass, where you can see your footprints in the trampled vegetation.

CHAPTER 11

About Rituals

Although Wiccan rituals are many and varied
and can be adapted for the seasons, the individual,
and magical intent, they all adhere to a basic format,
as outlined in this chapter. Since they can be performed with
friends just as well as singly, rituals are a great introduction to
magical group work, and this chapter explains how to work with
others, and even how to start a coven.

Re-enactment of mythological stories may also be included, and
whatever else suits the witch, or coven, performing the ritual. This
part of the book starts with a basic ritual that you can adapt to suit
yourself and includes rituals to mark the special occasions that
occur in all our lives. All of them can be easily adapted for group
work, too, and some rituals, especially life rituals, actually require
more than one person to perform them—you can't really marry
yourself in a handfasting!

A basic ritual

Prepare the space by tidying it and laying an altar, if you wish. Cleanse the area spiritually by smudging—burning sage and letting the smoke waft around the room—or using your besom (ritual broom) to sweep the area symbolically.

Prepare yourself by taking some time to relax. Maybe have a shower and visualize your troubles and everyday cares running away with the water. It's good to have a special ritual robe to wear, to signify that you are doing something magical, but this is not necessary.

You should always start with casting a circle, i.e. making a ritual space. Do this by lighting candles positioned for the four elements—earth equals north, air equals east, fire equals south, water equals west—or drawing a pentagram in the air with your athame, or simply with your hands, for each element, and then raising energy. You could do this by visualizing energy rising from the ground, Mother Earth, and coming down from the sky, Father Sun. See Chapter 9 for energy-raising meditations.

Honour the deities and give thanks. Light a candle to represent the gods and goddesses of your choice, or thank them by saying out loud any blessings they have given you recently.

Perform or renew any spells that you wish to do, bless new magical tools or gems by passing them through the elemental candles, and maybe do a meditation or divination. If you are with friends, re-enact a story from mythology.

Ground yourself by having something to eat and drink—this is called the "cakes and ale" part of the ritual, but any food and drink will do. If you are with others, this is a good time to chat to tell them about spiritual books you have read or to plan future meetings. If you are by yourself, take some time to think about what spiritual things you have done since your last ritual and what you plan to do by the next one. Ensure you leave a little drink in the bottom of the cup for the earth offering.

When you are done, close your magical circle by extinguishing the candles and any incense you may have lit, and thank the deities and spirits for their presence.

Give thanks to the Earth Mother again with the earth offering—pour the rest of the drink from the "cakes and ale" over a plant in your garden or on your windowsill. This liquid is said to be very potent magically, so try to pour it over magical plants, such as herbs you are growing for spells, or a holly bush.

Group rituals

You don't need to be in a coven to perform rituals, but this is one area where having a group to work with can help, because the group's combined magical energies will be stronger than an individual's. Also, you simply cannot do certain things by yourself, such as some energy raising, and performing 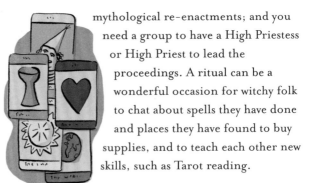 mythological re-enactments; and you need a group to have a High Priestess or High Priest to lead the proceedings. A ritual can be a wonderful occasion for witchy folk to chat about spells they have done and places they have found to buy supplies, and to teach each other new skills, such as Tarot reading.

INFORMAL GATHERING

You don't need a formal coven to perform a group ritual. Why not invite over some friends who are interested in magic, and perform a ritual together? If it goes well, make sure you read pages 130–34 about setting up your own study group or coven.

If you are writing a ritual for a group, make sure that everyone is comfortable with it, especially if you are new at working together; some people may feel strange about calling on certain deities or pantheons of deities, or be uncomfortable with doing a mythological re-enactment about a journey to the underworld where they meet death gods. Also ensure that the ritual is geared toward the level of experience of the participants, and that everyone is given something to do.

EVERYONE INVOLVED

Even if you write a ritual for more than a hundred people, you can involve everyone in some way—in energy raising, for example, with dancing, drumming, and chanting. Some people can bring food for the "cakes and ale" ceremony, and you can give others some seeds that they can plant while asking the blessing of the Earth Mother.

Blessing way

This is held for a pregnant woman before she gives birth, to strengthen her spiritually and emotionally, and to give her some much-needed calm before the chaos that is life with a newborn. It's a more spiritual version of a baby shower. One idea is to have a book in which guests can write suitable messages and advice, and poems. Those who wish can each say a blessing over the bump for a safe delivery and a healthy baby. You could ask everyone to bring a gemstone pebble and use them to make a necklace that will help the mother during pregnancy, birth, and beyond—a raw ruby for a safe pregnancy, a moonstone for confidence in her feminine power to birth, and amber for teething. Women who already have children often share their birth stories.

Entering womanhood

This ritual puts you in touch with the feminine divine, and the Goddess Hecate in particular, who can help you to decide what to do at life's crossroads. It is often used to celebrate a girl's first menstruation, when she becomes a woman. If she is thought to be mature enough, she may perform the ritual herself; otherwise, her mother does it on her behalf, and it is usually followed by a special outing or a treat.

First cast a circle. Fill your cauldron, or a big bowl, preferably dark in color, with water and put three candles in a triangle around it.

As you light the first candle, say:
"Hecate, I illuminate the past, so I may learn from it." As you light the second, say:
"Hecate, I illuminate the present, so I may live in it." As you light the third, say:

"Hecate, I illuminate the future, so I may grow into it."

Take your wand—willow is sacred to Hecate—or your athame and gently stir the water in the cauldron, saying:
"Hecate, wise crone, guider of women, guide me. Show me what I must see."

Then, watch the reflections of the candle flames in the cauldron for a response. You may see your own face, but older looking, symbolizing that you will become a leader of women; or you may see only two of the three candle flames, indicating you don't pay enough attention to whichever one you don't see. For example, if you don't see the first one's flame, it shows you are not learning from the past.

Welcoming a new baby

A naming ceremony is often held to welcome a newborn into the community, and usually outside so that Mother Nature can welcome the baby, too.

This means that the ritual may be delayed until the weather is warm enough; some parents wait until the child is three or four years old, so that he or she will have a memory of the event.

Witchy parents often keep the placenta—it can be easily frozen—and during the ceremony, plant a tree in the name of the child, with the placenta underneath it. Some serve it up as part of the party buffet, fried or as paté.

The parents ask close friends to guard the child and lead him or her to a good life; usually a woman (Goddess Mother) and a man (God Father) are chosen, but some parents choose four people, one for each element, instead.

Handfasting

Celebrations to mark an engagement and a wedding are called handfasting. An engagement handfasting usually lasts for a year and a day; others can be done to last until any children of the relationship are grown up, for life, or forever, in which case souls are joined so they are reborn together. Common elements in a handfasting are the unity candle—the bride and groom each carry a lighted candle to the altar and from them light a bigger candle; jumping the broom, which symbolizes starting a new life together; and binding the hands with a cord. Wedding rings are the everyday representation of the cord. If only coven members are present, the handfasting can be a completely Wiccan ritual, held in a forest glade or at home; if others attend, the ceremony may be more eclectic and the Wiccan parts less overt.

·Tip·

Some life rituals, such as a handfasting or a blessing way, may involve people who are not Wiccan. Be mindful of their sensibilities. For instance, consider including a lovely quote from the Bible or a historical poem for them to say. An email beforehand or a booklet on the day, explaining the different parts of the ritual, will make everyone more comfortable.

Rebirthing

When a quick ending and a new beginning are needed—perhaps to end an abusive relationship or to help you move far away—rebirthing rituals can help. Ideally, rebirthing rituals are done during an eclipse or at a blue moon—the second of two full moons in a calendar month, and a rare event—but they can be done when the moon is new. Light five differently colored candles, laid out in the shape of a pentagram—yellow or gold for the sun; green for earth and a positive future; blue or silver for the moon; black for protection; and white for light and positive energy. Meditate on the need for change, and what you are going to do in the mundane world to facilitate it. Ask your ancestors for help and also your patron deity or a lunar eclipse goddess, such as Rahu, Hecate, or Isis. Do this once a week until you feel comfortable with the changes you are making.

Croning

This ritual celebrates a woman reaching the third stage of life; post menopause, she is considered to be a wise woman or crone. Many women choose to declare that they are content with their age, and are proud of their laughter lines, at a croning. The woman is usually given a book with blank pages or signs up for a blog account, so she can record her knowledge for future generations. Younger female members of the family bring food to honor the crone, and listen to her stories, which may involve their births. She may be presented with white clothing, since there is no longer any danger of it being spoiled by menstrual blood, and, if she is part of a coven, a staff as a symbol of her wisdom and ability to guide the coven's younger members.

Death

Legally, the possibilities for a Wiccan burial are rather limited, although wonderful, ecologically sound forest burials are now allowed in some places. Witches prefer to celebrate life rather than to mourn death, and so the burial ceremony usually includes funny and inspiring stories being told about the dearly departed. The deceased's totem animal or guardian spirit is asked to accompany him or her to the other side, and a few coins may be left under the relevant statue, if there is one. After a cremation, the family or coven scatter the ashes at the departed's favorite outdoor ritual site, or throw them into the wind from the top of a hill or mountain.

CHAPTER 12

Seasonal Rituals

Wiccans have a working ritual called an Esbat
every Full Moon, and very six weeks or so, bigger
celebratory rituals called Sabbats are held. Four Sabbats are
astronomical, celebrating the longest night and day (solstices),
and the balance of night and day (equinoxes); and four are fire
festivals, because, traditionally, big bonfires were lit during
them. The rituals below can be adapted to your liking.

In the past, Esbats were held on the full moon
because communication was difficult and the rituals had
to be kept secret, but everyone knew when the full moon was.
As the power of the full moon lasts several days,
it is perfectly acceptable to have your ritual a couple
of days either side of the complete full moon, if that better
suits your work or family commitments.

An Esbat ritual

CIRCLE CASTING

"As above, so below, as without, so within, as the universe, so my soul, as the world, so my mind. The circle is cast and I am beyond the worlds, beyond the bounds of time, where night and day, birth and death, joy and sorrow meet as one."

CALLING THE QUARTERS

"From the North, I call forth Earth, which is Grounded Strength. Hail and welcome! From the East, I call forth Air, which is Clear Thought. Hail and welcome! From the South, I call forth Fire, which is Vital Spirit. Hail and welcome! From the West, I call forth Water, which is Intuitive Wisdom. Hail and welcome!"

INVOCATION TO THE GOD AND GODDESS

"O Goddess who rules the Earth and all within, who sets the time our lives begin, who brings me happiness and mirth, who gives me value and self-worth: touch this circle with your love, as below me, so above! O God of the Sun that shines above, who warms us with your light and love, who brings good health and prosperity and changes all as it should be: touch this circle with your love, as below me, so above!"

LIGHTING THE ALTAR CANDLE

"We light this candle today in presence of the Lord and Lady, without malice, without jealousy, without envy, without fear of aught beneath the setting sun, for we know that their light and love will guide us down the right path, even when we cannot see it, even in the darker times of winter ahead."

RITUAL WORKING

"This is the time of the Full Moon. This is a time for completion and positive magic; I am gathering my thoughts and power, wishes and desires for the coming month."

CAKES AND ALE

The partaking of food and drink is followed by releasing the quarters, deities, and circle by thanking them. This is basically the reverse of the above invocations.

Sabbats

Samhain, October 31

Decorate the altar with autumn leaves, photos of departed loved ones, a cauldron, a black altar cloth, bones, and carved pumpkins or turnips.

Samhain is the witchy New Year and last harvest festival. It is a great time to contact ancestors because the veil between the worlds is thin; you can also do divination. Set an extra space at dinner for spirit and ancestral visitors, and carve faces in turnips and pumpkins—scary ones to keep malevolent spirits away; happy ones to attract good spirits.

A Samhain ritual

CASTING THE CIRCLE

"I cast this circle once about, to keep all trouble and woe without. I cast this circle twice around, so that peace and love within it abound. With the third time this circle is now safe, protected by the might the Lord and Lady gave!"

INVOCATION OF THE GOD AND GODDESS

As you light their candles, or look into the sky, chant:

"Great Goddess, Dark Mother! I invite you to this circle to assist and protect me. Great God, God of the universal cycle of birth, death, and rebirth! I invite you to my circle to assist and protect me."

CALLING THE QUARTERS

As you light element candles, chant:

"To the element and spirits of Earth, I call upon your wisdom and ask for your energy to witness this celebration of this passing year, blessings to Samhain and union of spirit."

"To the element and spirits of Air, I call upon your wisdom and ask for your energy to clear communications with spirit, and divine knowledge and understanding."

"To the element and spirits of Fire, I call upon your wisdom and ask for your energy for purification of mind, body, spirit and the harvest. We ask for your divine protection over all things that we bring forth for review, reassessment, and resolution."

"To the element and spirits of Water, I call upon your wisdom and ask for your energy for examination of my path and progress."

LIGHTING THE ALTAR CANDLE

Either light the candle or hold a symbol of the season, and say: "*On this night of Samhain, I mark the Sun King's passing into the Land of the Young, and with it I note the passing of all who have gone before and all who will go after. Gracious Goddess, Mother of us all, teach me to know that in the time of the greatest darkness there is greatest light. Welcome winter, waning season! With night the new year comes; warm blessings be on those who bide with me, my family, friends, and indeed on all the world.*"

☗ · TIP · ☗

Don't be afraid to contact your ancestors at this time of year, or at a new moon. But always invite them, never force them to attend you; ghosts like respect just as much as living people!

CAKES AND ALE BLESSING

"*On this eve of Samhain I wish to honour and share my bounty. I offer this food and this drink and ask the Lord and Lady to accept them as my offering of honour and thanksgiving.*"

THANKING THE LORD AND LADY

As you blow out the God and Goddess candles, say:

"*I thank you, Great Goddess and great God, for attending my circle and for your gifts of love and protection.*"

DISMISSING THE QUARTERS

Blow out the candles and say:

"*To the element and spirits of Water, I thank you for your wisdom, and for your energy for examination of my path and progress. Hail and Farewell!*"

"*To the element and spirits of Fire, I thank you for your wisdom, and for your energy for purification of mind, body, spirit and the harvest. Hail and Farewell!*"

"*To the element and spirits of Air, I thank you for your wisdom, and for your energy in clearing communications to spirit and giving me divine knowledge and understanding. Hail and Farewell!*"

"*To the element and spirits of Earth, I thank you for your wisdom, and for your energy and love in witnessing this celebration of the passing year. Hail and Farewell!*"

CLOSING THE CIRCLE

"*May the love of the Lady and the joy of the Lord be ever in my heart. This circle is open and yet is unbroken. Merry meet, merry part, and merry meet again!*"

Yule, circa December 21

Decorate the altar with pine cones, garlands of cranberries and popcorn (great as an earth offering for the birds later), lots of candles, christmas tree baubles in red and gold, mistletoe, symbols of the Moon. Yule celebrates the rebirth of the Sun God, often portrayed as the Holly King, who symbolizes cold and winter and is overcome by the Oak King, who symbolizes strength and warmth. Bake cookies to share and give as presents. This is a time for meditation on rebirth, quiet reflection, and getting up to greet the sun at dawn.

Imbolc, February 1

Decorate the altar with unlit candles, seeds, things in threes to symbolize the triple goddess—Maiden, Mother, Crone.

This is the Goddess Brighid's festival, so recite poetry, make a Brighid's Cross, bless your candles for the year—this Sabbat is also called Candlemas—and learn about healing or perform some healing for others, such as reiki or making herbal tea.

Ostara, circa March 21

Decorate the altar with a besom (for symbolic spring cleaning), decorated eggs, spring greenery, rabbit statue.

A Sabbat of balance and fertility—the Sun God is reborn about nine months later; clean out old magical herbs, give away witchy books and things you no longer need, and make plans for the coming fertile season, physically and spiritually.

Beltaine, May 1

Decorate the altar with fresh flowers in pastel colors, symbols of togetherness, such as a photo of a happy couple or two fish in a bowl, a mini maypole or other phallic symbol.

This is a big fire festival and a celebration of couples. Light a fire if you can—a bonfire in the yard, a small home fire in a fireplace, or a mini fire in your cauldron; braid different coloured ribbons together for decoration and magic; make a floral crown or daisy chain to wear.

Litha, circa June 22

Decorate the altar with sun symbols, such as a sunflower, sun-shaped candle holders, and with acorns and saffron.

This is the main Sabbat to honor the Sun God, and so the festival is about virility, strength, and courage. Have a picnic or hold an outdoor meditation; do a ritual or meditate at midday; perform energy-raising meditations and activities.

Lughnasadh or Lammas, August 1

Decorate the altar with freshly harvested grain and vegetables, sheaves of corn and wheat, a sword or a new athame.

This is the first harvest festival and a time of great joy and fun, often seen as the witchy Thanksgiving. Make corn dollies, play "lughnasy games" (silly childish games), tell jokes, bake bread, and make jewelry with metal wire.

A Lughnasadh ritual

Prepare your sacred space as you wish, by casting a circle and raising energy. Light your altar candle and say:

"Here I am on the first harvest, the sacred festival of Lughnasadh, seeking to understand life, death, and rebirth and to honour those who have endured each. Lord and Lady, give me insight!"

Spend some time in quiet reflection on life, and the bounty Mother Earth gives us with the harvest. Place some food or harvest items on your altar and say:

"I thank you, Mother Earth, for the bounty you give us! I thank you, gods and goddesses, for your guidance and protection.

(Add specific instances from the last year here if you like.)

As my goddess matures and her pregnant belly grows, so the harvest grows. The Sun God is waning, but his energy still warms my body and his strength strengthens my mind. I give you both this share of my harvest as a token of my thanks."

🕯 · **TIP** · 🕯

Use altar decorations, such as the food from this ritual, as an earth offering after the ritual is finished, to give back to Mother Earth by feeding her creatures.

Take a feather, preferably a colorful one, such as from a peacock or an iridescent, black magpie feather, and lightly tickle your cheek with it. Smile and say:

"Lord Lugh, Lady Gaia, come to me! The joy in everything help me see! I may be stressed, but today I'll have fun—enjoy my food, and party with the sun!"

If anyone in your family is sad, or a friend takes things too seriously, or a work colleague is under stress, visualize that person and then imagine tickling him or her with your feather until they laugh.

Close the sacred space as you wish.

Mabon, circa September 22

Decorate the altar with berries, root vegetables, symbols of balance, such as a scale or a ying-yang drawing, and apples.

This is the second harvest festival, a time of balance and preparing for the introspective winter. Celebrate with fortune telling, canning and preserving fruit and vegetables, making your own mead, and baking corn cakes.

ᛒ ·TIPS· ᛒ

There are many witchy activities you can share with friends who are not witches, or children with whom you do not want to talk about magic yet:

Samahain
Carve pumpkins or make paper lanterns with colorful paper; visit the grave of departed loved ones.

Yule
Decorate a Christmas tree, evergreen symbol of hope, with gold baubles to symbolize the Sun God; make a chocolate Yule log.

Imbolc
Make your own candles; have a poetry competition; feed birds and other outdoor animals in return for Mother Earth feeding you during harvest time.

Ostara
Decorate eggs; have a swap party where everyone brings make-up or clothes they no longer want. Anything left can go to a charity shop.

Beltaine
Have a dance party; visit a farm or zoo with baby animals; plant vegetables or flowers.

Litha
Hold an outdoor family picnic. In my coven, we take this as an opportunity to invite and get to know the non-Wiccan partners of coven members.

Lughnasadh
Play silly games, or have strength competitions; bake bread and share it with neighbors; make funny masks with sticks and grains.

Mabon
Bake together, have a pot-luck party; volunteer for a charity to share your good luck with those less fortunate.

CHAPTER 13

Continuing Your Journey

Before joining a coven, first explore by yourself,
both intellectually and spiritually, so that you can do
your magic and worship exactly when and how
you want, and learn which tradition of Wicca and
which pantheon of deities work for you. How long this
solitary time takes depends on you. Some people totally
immerse themselves and feel ready to join a coven
after a few months. Some take years, and some prefer
to remain solitary. If and when you do finally
join a coven, you will be able to tell the good, solid
covens from those who are just trying to be "cool,"
and you will know what you want from a coven and
what you can bring to it.

·TIP·

Be wary of covens that are willing, or even require, you to go through initiation at the first or second meeting. A good coven will take its time to see if you are a suitable fit, and will allow you to take some time, too.

Moots and study groups

A good way to start mixing with other Wiccans is to meet socially at moots. These are witchy gatherings held in bars or community centers. A specific topic is usually discussed for an hour or so, and then everyone just mingles. You can find listings of these online (see Resources, page 140), or check the noticeboards of your local New Age and health food stores.

You might find a study group in the same way. These groups often meet monthly in a café to discuss a witchy book, a mythological story, or a type of magic, such as candle spells, gemstone magic, or thanksgiving rituals. Attending a study group gives you the freedom to practice how you want, rather than following the ideas or traditions of a coven, which may not suit you exactly, but still enables you to learn from others.

After a few meetings, you may be invited to celebrate the main Sabbats with other witches in a semi-public gathering, which often arises from a moot or a study group, and from there, an invitation to join a coven might follow.

Joining a coven

Treat the initial steps of joining a coven like a date with a stranger—meet in a public place and ask a lot of questions. Do not be pressured into doing things you do not wish to do, but be aware that just because you are uncomfortable with something right now, does not mean it is wrong. For example, many traditional Wiccan covens practice skyclad. If you are uncomfortable with this, examine whether this is due to the people involved, or whether it is a block within yourself that with some more solitary study, you may overcome.

🕯 · TIP · 🕯

When the weather is warm, consider a hike or a picnic for your
new witchy group. Both will bring all of you closer to nature, and you
can do a simple ritual or meditation even in a busy place,
dressed in street clothes.

QUESTIONS

You need information when deciding whether or not to join a coven.
Here are some suggestions for questions to ask.

- When and where do you meet, and how often? Their schedule may not suit you due to work or family obligations, or because you don't drive and cannot get there.
- Which deities or pantheon do you worship? Is it okay if I worship different deities at home?
- Am I required to bring anything to coven meetings? A coven may meet in a hired room, with everyone contributing a small amount toward the cost; or everyone may bring some food to share, or some candles once a quarter.
- When do you initiate new members? Immediately upon joining the coven, after a year and a day, whenever the new coven member is ready …?
- What if I can't attend all coven meetings? In some covens, you need to attend three out of four, or at least every second meeting, or you may be removed.
- Do you have any special training or tasks a new member must do? In some covens, the new member must stay late to clean up, or meet the High Priestess once a month for one-on-one tuition.
- What happens next? When can I meet the whole coven? Some covens will have you meet the High Priestess and/or High Priest several times before meeting the coven. In some covens, new members attend Sabbats only for the first year, and are allowed to be present at Esbats—where more advanced magic is done—only after they are initiated.

Starting your own magical group

Some people work well by themselves, and never want to join a coven or other magical group, except maybe online support or distance group work. Others find it easier to learn in a coven, or crave the social aspect of a magical group. The easiest thing is to join an established coven, but they can be difficult to find, especially outside of big cities. Those covens you do find may already have too many members, or the "vibes" you feel may indicate they are not right for you. What do you do then? Do what I did early in my witchy career— start your own magical group! It requires time and energy, but carries great rewards.

Don't just read a couple of books about covens, although there are some good ones (see page 140), and start a group with big initiation ceremonies and your own embroidered robes! Start slowly and, like Mother Earth when she allows a mighty oak to grow from a small acorn, start small.

First, find some people who have the same magical vision as you do. This may not be your best friend, even if she is into witchcraft. When I decided I wanted to form a coven, I first thought of my three best friends, with whom I had been doing guided meditation and attending Tarot lessons. But it turned out that one of them wasn't really committed outside of a fun hobby, one was Christian and so didn't want to worship other deities, and one was very interested, but only wanted to worship Egyptian deities, whereas I felt drawn to Celtic gods and goddesses. So I put the word out that I was going to form a magical study group, via friends of friends, a notice in the New Age shop, and online. We met twice a month in a local café to discuss a magical subject. The public place meant everyone was comfortable, and we could get to know each other. From that group, I found some people who were on the same

CIRCLE OF ENERGY

In a beginner's coven, or simply with a group of people interested in spirituality, my favorite way of raising energy is to hold hands in a circle. One person—the High Priestess if it is a coven—starts by gently squeezing the hand of the person to her left, who then squeezes the next person's hand and so on. Start off slowly and each time a circle of hand-squeezing is completed, go a bit faster, while visualizing a cone of energy building in the circle. When the High Priestess feels enough energy has been raised, she lets go of the hands on either side of her and raises her hands up high. Everyone else does the same, and then the ritual proper begins.

wavelength as I am, and we started meeting privately. We decided on a name for the coven and some basic ground rules, some of which I took from my mentor's coven (she had moved to France), some of which we got from books, and some we came up with ourselves. Usually, a coven meets every Full Moon for an Esbat (ritual) and for the eight annual Sabbats (festivals). We started off meeting just for the Sabbats, and continuing with the study group in between those festivals, again so we could get used to each other slowly. Sabbats tend to focus on celebration and worship more than on

heavy magic, which may be difficult to concentrate upon in the presence of lots of people you don't know. A couple of people fell away as things got more serious, and I was left with five members, who became the core group, and truly dear spiritual friends.

I was young when I started my coven and unsure if I wanted to take on the spiritual and emotional commitment. I wanted to join an established coven and learn from them, but looking back, the Goddess guided me, and I wouldn't want my life to be any different from the way it is now.

Involving your pets in magic

I think my readers know enough about witchcraft to realize that not all witches have a black cat. A surprising number of us do, though. Witches love nature and tend to love animals. Black cats have the most difficulty finding a new home when they end up in a shelter, and many witches give preference to a black cat or dog when adopting. But animals are not just companions for a lonely evening; they can also be companions in magic.

Some pets have an affinity for magic, and want actively to help with spells or rituals. They have the potential to be a familiar, i.e. a creature who channels animal spirits to assist in rituals, the way humans ask fairies or deities to be present. The familiar can also lend its magical energy to a spell to make it more powerful.

The best way to "train" animals is to let them be present when you work a spell or do a ritual, even if they are disruptive, as they can be, especially to begin with. My cat, Piggy, was a familiar. He started out wanting to play with the tassles on my robe, but quickly learned to walk the circle with me at the beginning of a ritual, and would mew in each direction as I called the quarters. He was also very interested in Tarot cards. At first, I thought he just wanted to play with them, but by paying close attention to what he actually did, I figured out that he was choosing cards for me, especially when I did a reading for myself, or about a new spell I had written. I always do a divination for my new spells to see if they are any good or if there is a potential problem. (See also page 81.)

Cats and dogs are not the only creatures with the potential to be familiars. Any animal you have a close connection with can help with magic. A horse, given reasonably free rein to carry you on its back, may take you to a forest glade that is ideal for meditation, or a tree from which you can take a branch to make a wand. An iguana can sit on your altar and be a visual focus for your magic; two goldfish in the north quarter of your home will help attract money and abundance from earth, the element of the north; and a pair of any animal kept in the south (for fire and passion) will assist in bringing love to your home, and keeping it there.

When not to use magic

Magical energy is all around us, but that doesn't mean it is always a good idea to harness it. Indeed, your magic may not be welcome when it targets someone else. Always ask if it is OK to do a spell for someone, unless you already know that person approves of magic. If you are afraid of asking, you probably have your answer. You can still send people positive energy, which is similar to praying, or pray to whichever deities and spirits you believe in.

Magic for health and healing, for yourself and others, is a good example of where you need to tread carefully. Many healing spells and magical recipes are strong and work well, even something as simple as visualizing yourself in a healing bubble of blue light, or carrying a turquoise stone with you to avoid broken bones. But magic tends to take a while to incubate, and in that time an illness could take a stronger hold in your body, so always make sure the health issue you are working magic for is nothing serious, and if you remotely suspect it is, go to see a doctor as well as (or before) doing a spell. Also, sometimes there is an underlying reason behind someone's illness, so they can have some introspective time or rest; so be especially careful when doing health magic to help others.

Love magic is another tricky one. While you are entitled to find love, you are not entitled to compromise someone else's free will by using magic to make him or her fall in love with you, even if you are sure that person is perfect for you. I recommend keeping the love spell neutral by asking for love to come to you; while you may hope that the magic will attract a specific person, you keep your mind and heart open for anyone. The other way is to add a caveat, such as "if it be for the best of all, and the harm of none, so may it be done!"

Lastly, don't become too reliant on While it can certainly help in most cases, it cannot solve all our problems. You need to work in both the mundane and magical worlds to solve your problems and attain your goals.

Tables of Magical Associations

SPELL INTENT

	Love	Sex	Fertility	Work	Money	Protection	Friendship	Curse-breaking
Crystal	Rose quartz	Garnet	Emerald	Tiger's eye	Malachite	Amethyst	Amber	Onyx
Color	Pink	Red	Green	Brown	Gold	White	Yellow	Black
God	Eros	Pan	Amun	Lugh	Ra	Atlas	Baldr	Osiris
Goddess	Aphrodite	Venus	Cerridwen	Demeter	Oshun	Artemis	Hestia	Persephone
Primary herb	Cinnamon	Red peppercorn	Mandrake	Irish moss	Basil	Clove	Valerian	Bergamot

COLORS AND THEIR MAGICAL CORRESPONDENCES

	Pink	Red	Dark red	Light green	Dark green	Pale brown	Brown	Gold	White
Primary magic	Love	Sex	Warding	Changing attitudes	Prosperity	Travel	Work	Money	Peace
Secondary magic	Harmony	Passion	Vigor	Weather	Fertility	Building	Animals	Beauty	Purificatio
Herb	Red clover	Chili	Red	Feverfew	Irish moss	Ginger	Mandrake	Pennyroyal	Camomile

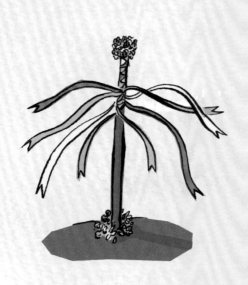

THE ELEMENTS AND THEIR MAGICAL CORRESPONDENCES

	Earth	Air	Fire	Water
Direction	North	East	South	West
Color	Brown	Yellow	Red	Blue
Crystal	Tiger's eye	Diamond	Opal	Aquamarine
Magical tool	Pentagram	Wand	Athame	Chalice
Season	Fall	Spring	Summer	Winter
Animal	Stag	Birds	Salamander	Fish
Altar symbol	Salt	Incense	Candle	Water
Time of day	Morning	Dawn	Noon	Night
God	Cernunnos	Toth	Loki	Poseidon
Goddess	Demeter	Arianrhod	Brigit	Venelia
Magic	Inner strength	Intuition	Energy	Cleansing

Luck	Justice	Health	Confidence	Fairies	Ancestors
Obsidian	Topaz	Turquoise	Clear quartz	Moonstone	Hematite
Silver	Orange	Blue	Dark blue	Rainbow	Gray
Odin	Forseti	Apollo	Zeus	Loki	Anubis
Athena	Maat	Brigit	Isis	Morrigan	Arianrhod
Nutmeg	Verveine	Camomile	Tarragon	Thistle	Lemon balm

Yellow	Black	Silver	Orange	Blue	Dark blue	Gray	Purple	Lavender
Friendship	Curse-breaking	Luck	Justice	Health	Confidence	Ancestors	Occult knowledge	Psychic awareness
Exams	Protection	Gambling	Leadership	Home	Wisdom protection	Patience	Power	Blessing
Citronella	Black	Eyebright	Oregano	Rosemary	Thistle	Sage	Chives	Lavender

DAYS OF THE WEEK

	Monday	Tuesday	Wednesday	Thursday	Friday	Saturday	Sunday
Magic	Healing	Power	Divination	Money	Love	Protection	Happiness
Deity	Moon	Mars	Mercury	Jupiter	Venus	Saturn	Sun
Color	Silver	Red	Purple	Blue	Pink	Gray	Gold
Crystal	Opal	Ruby	Amethyst	Sapphire	Rose quartz	Quartz crystal	Carnelian
Herb	Fennel	Chili	Eyebright	Basil	Cinnamon	Clove	Star anise

MOON PHASES

	New moon	Waxing	Full moon	Waning
Magic	Meditation	Prosperity	Thanksgiving	Protection
Goddess aspect	Death	Maiden	Mother	Crone
God	Osiris	Hermes	Lugh	Balor
Goddess	Artemis	Diana	Cerridwen	Hecate
Sabbat	Yule	Beltaine	Litha	Samhain

Glossary

Athame A ritual knife that is not used to cut things physically, but for magic and working with energy, such as dipping the tip of the blade in a bowl of herbs on the altar to charge them with magical energy for future use in spells or medicinal teas. Traditionally has a black handle.
Astral plane A different plane of existence from that inhabited by humans, said to be where spirits live.

Besom Witch's broom Often decorated with cleansing herbs, such as sage, parsley, and rosemary to cleanse the ritual space symbolically before working magic, or decorated with herbs and flowers to look pretty for a handfasting.
Bolline Knife used to cut things used for magic, such as herbs or cord. Traditionally has a white handle.
Book of Shadows A diary for a witch to write down spells and magic; often kept online these days. Abbreviated to BoS.

Cauldron A large pot or bowl, traditionally black, used to make magical foods and for water-scrying.
Cleansing Spiritual cleaning, removing negativity.
Coven A group of witches working magic together regularly.

Deosil Clockwise direction.
Divination Reading the future with tarot cards, runes, or other methods.

Esbat Coven meeting, usually at a full moon.

Familiar Animal, often a pet, who helps in magic.

Grimoire *See* Book of Shadows.
Grounding Releasing excess energy after magic.

Handfasting Wiccan wedding.
Highpriest/ess Coven leader and teacher.

Joss stick Incense in stick form, usually bought rather than homemade.

Ointment A semi-solid medical preparation used to soothe the head or skin.

Pagan Originally any believer in non-monotheistic religion, but these days usually means a believer in Earth-based spirituality (Wiccan, Druid, Shaman, etc).
Pantheon A group of deities associated with a particular culture, such as the Celtic pantheon or Greek pantheon.
Patron deity A deity you feel especially close to.
Pentacle A five-pointed star in a circle; sometimes a five-petalled flower is used to symbolize this on the altar, or a pentagram made from stalks of herbs.
Pentagram A five-pointed star without a circle; although often used interchangeably with pentacle.
Psychic A person who is extremely sensitive to energies and otherwordly entities.

Rede/Wiccan rede The basic Wiccan moral standpoint: "And it harm none, do as thou wilt."

Sabbat Major Wiccan festival There are eight each year, beginning with October 31 and Samhain, through Yule, Imbolc, Ostara, Beltane, Litha, Lammas, and Mabon.
Salve *See* ointment.
Scrying Form of divination done by looking in a pool of water, crystal ball, mirror, etc.
Sygil A magical symbol, often personally designed.
Skyclad Naked for the purpose of ritual magic.

Talisman A magical amulet.

Visualization Imagining something in your mind's eye. Also used for very deep meditation.

Warding Protecting something magically.
Widdershins Counterclockwise.

Useful Resources

Follow Silja on twitter at @witchsilja to learn more about spells and her magical life. Silja's books *The Green Wiccan Herbal* and *The Green Wiccan Year* are also available from CICO Books.

WEBSITES

www.aquariantabernaclechurch.org: Great American Wiccan website.

www.circlesanctuary.org: Circle Sanctuary is author and famous Wiccan Selena Fox's website and organization. with information on life rituals, events, interfaith work, and more.

www.cog.org: Covenant of the Goddess: This mostly US-based group works on getting legal recognition for Wicca and is very active in networking.

www.paganfed.org: The Pagan Federation—an international organization, UK based, that runs witchy events and also has a great magazine.

www.sacred-texts.com: Religious and spiritual texts, including Wiccan, Druid, and ancient Shaman.

www.thealmanack.com: A calendar-style website with current moon phases, planets that rule the day, etc. Has a handy monthly printable page.

www.witchcraft.org: The Children of Artemis— UK-based organization with an informative website. They also run witchy gatherings and conventions, and publish a magazine.

www.witchvox.com: Extensive Wiccan site, international in scope but concentrates on the US.

BIBLIOGRAPHY

HISTORY AND MODERN FORMS OF WITCHCRAFT AND WICCA
Lost Gods of Albion: The Chalk Hill Figures of Britain Paul Newman (Sutton Publishing, 1999)
The Triumph of the Moon: A History of Modern Pagan Witchcraft Ronald Hutton (Oxford Paperbacks, 1995)
Stations of the Sun: A History of the Ritual Year in Britain Ronald Hutton (Oxford Paperbacks, 2001)
What Thou Wilt: Traditional and Innovative Trends in Post-Gardnerian Witchcraft Jon Hanna (Evertype, 2010)

WORKING IN GROUPS OR COVENS
Coven Craft Amber K (Llewellyn Publications, 2002)
Hedge Witch: A Guide to Solitary Witchcraft Rae Beth (Robert Hale Ltd, 1992)
Inside a Witches' Coven Edain McCoy (Llewellyn Publications, 2003)
Practical Wicca and Witchcraft: Towards the Wiccan Circle Sorita d'Este (Avalonia, 2008)
The Real Witches' Coven Kate West (Element Publishing, 2003)
Wicca: A Guide for the Solitary Practitioner Scott Cunningham (Llewellyn Publications, 1988)
A Witches' Bible: The Complete Witches' Handbook Janet and Stewart Farrar (Robert Hale Ltd, 2002)

OTHER INTERESTING BOOKS
The Alchemist and the Tea Cup: A complete guide to tea leaf reading Oein DeBhairduin (Llwellyn Publishing, 2011)
The Ancient British Goddess: Goddess Myths, Legends, Sacred Sites and Present Revelation Kathy Jones (Ariadne Publications, 2001)
Cunningham's Encyclopedia of Magical Herbs Scott Cunningham (Llewellyn Publications, 2000)
Encyclopedia of Celtic Wisdom: A Celtic Shaman's Sourcebook Caitlin and John Matthews (Element, 1994)

Index